Dr. Moore's
Reading and Writing Series

New Aesop's Fable Scripts

Drama Resources
for Multi-Skills Classrooms

....
Dr. Kenneth H. Moore
....

We Mean
BOOKS

Endorsements

This book stands out amongst thousands of books made for teaching non-native speakers English as a second or foreign language. This book is unique not only because there are not many English textbooks that use Aesop's Fables, Reader's Theatre, or systematic learning objectives that require learners' creative thinking skills and knowledge about people such as this book does. It stands out not only because it uses well known stories with interesting and abundant moral values that could lead many people to see with diverse perspectives (which has been acknowledged by many ELT related scholars and practitioners as an effective method for learning language). It is unique, moreover, not only because it provides clear language objectives with many activities that elicit learners' cognition, emotions, and creative thinking skills (an aspect seldom found in other ELT related materials) or because of its applicability in Korean contexts and anywhere in this world. Out of all the strengths of this book mentioned here, perhaps the one that says the most to me is that it was written by Dr. Kenneth Moore, who not only has profound knowledge and experience of teaching teachers who teach English as a second or foreign language, but also has a humanitarian personality which focuses on understanding what people need to have as teachers and as humans living in this competitive and inhuman world. As one of many people who are lucky to have encountered such a wonderful person as Dr. Kenneth Moore, I cannot find a better word that can sufficiently describe how good this book is and how lucky we are to have this book than this: Wow!! Congratulations to Dr. Moore! Congratulations to the users of this book!

Professor Kang Nam-Joon
Sookmyung Women's University

I love this book as an ESL instructor. Although there are multiple scripts of Aesop's Fables for elementary school students, it is hard to find a proper one for high-leveled students. The strength of this book is that it suggests very specific ways to lead the class for teachers, and it will be very helpful for all of us.

Lee Hyang, English Education Consultant

The direct translation is "This book serves as good guidance for an exam-free semester which emphasizes student-led activities and students' active involvement in the classroom. It also offers chances for students to cultivate cooperative attitudes and desirable relationships."

Kang Seo Yeon, Middle School Teacher

Dr. Moore's New Aesop's Fable Scripts will be helpful for students and teachers because it has easy, fun, and moral scripts as well as pre and post activities… This is a good resource for English teachers planning for free school semester, English club, afternoon class, and correlated curriculum-class-test. And students who are bored in the English classroom can find that English is a cool tool for communication through this book.

Lee Kyoung Hee, High School Teacher

Dr. Moore was my language acquisition theories and writing professor and he guided Korean English teachers including me passionately to the light house of English writing and theories of teaching English step by step. It was such a great opportunity for me to rebuild my writing skills and language theories more systematically after I became a teacher.

I was so happy to hear that he published this book because I have been thirsty of this kind of teaching drama text book as an English teacher for a long time and I am so honored to write some comment.

First of all, this book attracts student's interest because they are familiar with the Aesop's fables and young learners like to perform drama in the class. Teachers can engage students naturally as they become familiar with English Grammar and various vocabulary items and idioms while using this book. This book will be very useful for teachers and self- study learners as well because it has very systematic contents like pre-reading, script and post reading activities. Self-study learners will be able to easily follow the sequence of the book and will be exposed to some great colloquial English expressions and idioms.

                              Kang Moon Sook, Elementary School Teacher

It has not been easy to teach students English literature in Korean education system. Accordingly, I used to deal with literature as just a type of text reading. After 2015 Textbook Revision where English literature reading has been adopted, however, I have come to think about how to teach it in class. As even teacher's guides do not provide clear instructions, this book will be extremely beneficial for both in-service teachers and many students who want to study literature. Specifically, the book gave great ideas about how I can relate each literary work to a variety of activities in regard of their levels of difficulty. I sincerely look forward to the next series.

Park Yu Min, High School Teacher

Table of Contents

Preface

Introduction

Chapter 1 Belling the Cat

Chapter 2 The Shepherd Boy and the Wolf

Chapter 3 The North Wind and the Sun

Chapter 4 The Rabbit and the Turtle

Chapter 5 The Lion and the Mouse

Chapter 6 The Man, the Boy, and the Donkey

Chapter 7 The Grasshopper and the Ants

Chapter 8 Androcles and the Lion

Chapter 9 Writing Our Own Scripts

Appendix 1 Performance Notes

Appendix 2 Extension Ideas

Bibliography

Preface

This book is intended to provide English teachers with engaging and useful drama resources to develop their students' language skills and creativity. It grew out of my nine years' experience as a professor in a teacher-training program in Seoul. My students were mostly in service Korean English teachers from Seoul or Gyeonggi-do. As part of my writing course, my students would write original Reader's Theater scripts based on Aesop's Fables and/or Folk Stories, perform them in front of their classmates, and then engage in reflections on their work. This was an enjoyable exercise for both me and my students, and gave rise to many creative and engaging scripts.

    Through the experience of teaching this course, I became convinced that Reader's Theater could be an invaluable resource for language teachers from both a motivational and a language-learning perspective. I therefore undertook to write eight original Reader's Theater scripts in conversational, idiomatic English based on Aesop's Fables and to provide Pre-reading and Extension Activities to go with each script. I chose to base the scripts on Aesop's Fables because Aesop's Fables are short and have a clear story centered on a lesson that is universally understandable and relevant. Thus students can easily make an emotional connection between the story and their own experiences, and also use the story to develop critical thinking skills and emotional intelligence as they discuss how to apply the story or its lesson to their real lives. Each script also focuses on certain grammatical features, vocabulary items, and common idioms and expressions.

I would like to thank the following people for their invaluable assistance in helping me complete this project: my editor Min Gi Hong for her guidance and insightful comments; my wife Jean Kyoung Kim for her support and motivation; the colleagues who shared my interest in Reader's Theater;[1] and most of all, the many dedicated Korean English teachers that I have taught and learned from during the past nine years. It has been a pleasure and a privilege.

---

[1] I developed RT courses in collaboration with Erik Figueroa and Matthew Walker and collaborated with Erik Figueroa on "Reader's Theater in Mixed-Skills Classrooms: Guidelines for Writing Effective Reader's Theater Scripts," KOTESOL International Conference, October 21, 2012.

Introduction

Reader's Theater

Reader's Theater is an accessible way to do drama in class with minimal preparation. It can be used to support other lessons and does not require extensive stage sets, costumes, full memorization, or elaborate blocking and rehearsal (Shepard, 2004). Readers customarily stand in front of the class and read from a script with their own parts marked or highlighted. Students are encouraged to speak clearly and confidently, to look at the audience, and to convey the emotion that is appropriate to their character's personality and dramatic situation.

Reader's Theater has many clear benefits for language learners in that it provides comprehensible input in the form of conversational, idiomatic English, facilitates noticing of grammatical and lexical features, and provides opportunities for language production and fluency development. Furthermore, as students become actively involved in drama, they are required to use visual, auditory, and physical learning channels, and naturally gravitate to the one that suits them best (Desiatova, 2009), thus making drama a valuable resource for developing and respecting students' multiple intelligences.

In addition to developing and respecting students' multiple intelligences and individual learning styles, Reader's Theater offers a way to motivatestudents and engage them in a lesson as they improve their reading, speaking, and listening skills. Moreover, a Reader's Theater lesson provides differentiated instruction that can involve learners at all skill levels. Finally, the scripts in this book and the Extension Projects that accompany them are designed to help students develop Social and Emotional Intelligence, Creativity, and Critical Thinking Skills.

The Theory behind this Book

• **Comprehensible input**   Steven Krashen has proposed the Comprehension Hypothesis, which states that people "acquire language when we understand messages, when we understand what people tell us and when we understand what we read" (2004). Consisting mainly of dialogue, Reader's Theater scripts expose students to conversational, idiomatic English (input) and involve students in active reading and listening, helping to make input comprehensible through meaningful context.

• **Noticing**   Richard Schmidt has proposed the Noticing Hypothesis, which states that learners must notice, or have conscious awareness of, features of the target language so that those features can be taken into the learner's developing second language system (1990). One factor that facilitates noticing is frequency – the more often learners are exposed to a form, the more likely they are to notice it. Students must read with understanding and correct pronunciation and are given opportunities to notice lexical and grammatical features, both through repetition in the text itself and through repetition in rehearsal. Due to the collaborative nature of the activity and the engaging nature of the material, students will read through a text several times (frequency) without becoming bored.

• **The Lexical Approach**   This approach to language learning and teaching also emphasizes noticing. Proponents of the Lexical Approach recognize that a great percentage of language consists of collocations and lexical chunks (expressions and idioms), and they propose that teachers should devote some time to helping students notice and become aware of language as it is actually used in authentic texts (Lewis, 2000). The Grammar and Vocabulary Focus section of each chapter points out grammatical forms, vocabulary, and expressions in the Readers' Theater scripts that teachers can help students to notice. Through a Reader's Theater performance, students get a sense of how grammatical patterns and lexical chunks and collocations work in an authentic context.

- **Output** Merrill Swain's Output Hypothesis states that pushing learners to produce written and spoken output is facilitative of language acquisition, leading to increased fluency, noticing of grammatical forms, and language processing (Swain, 1995). Actively reading the scripts can help students master the phonological aspects of the language and gain confidence in using English. The collaborative nature of the rehearsal encourages more production: discussions about performance, meaning, and form (metatalk). The Writing and Discussion Projects section provides more opportunities for meaningful written and/or spoken production.

- **Motivation** Reader's Theater is motivating for students. They work collaboratively and can personalize the text as they become involved in the characters and the relevance of the story's theme. Reader's Theater is also scaffolded: no language production or memorization is required for the actual performance, so even lower-level students can participate and experience success. A Reader's Theater lesson provides variety in the classroom, and students have opportunities to use different learning styles and intelligences. The Writing and Discussion Projects section provides meaningful, collaborative production opportunities and helps students think and reflect on the lesson of the fable, express their own opinions about it, and apply the lesson to their own lives. All of these features have been linked to increased motivation in the classroom (Zoltán Dörnyei, 2001).

- **Critical Thinking and Creativity** Here is Bloom's Revised Taxonomy of human cognition, arranged from lowest to highest thinking skills: Remember, Understand, Apply, Analyze, Evaluate, and Create (David Sousa, 2006). Most reading comprehension questions in textbooks do not move beyond the most fundamental aspects of cognition – they merely check students' factual knowledge or basic understanding of the material (Remember and Understand in Bloom's Revised Taxonomy). The After Reading Activities that require students to compare animals and humans, to reflect on how the characters might feel, or to create personal analogies can help students to develop their creativity and to engage meaningfully with the Target Language. The After Performance Questions require students to use higher-level thinking skills as they apply the material in the script to a new situation, analyze the material to see how the parts make up the whole, or evaluate the material based on some criteria. The Writing and Discussion Projects also give students opportunities to develop their creativity though group projects such as "retell the fable in a school setting." The activities in this sections are designed to allow students to creatively relate the fable's lesson to their own lives and value-systems, and also to the world at large. Create - to use the material to make something new – is the highest level of Bloom's Taxonomy. As Eun-ok Ahn points out, much educational research has shown that creativity-enhancing activities not only increase student motivation, but also help them to become better problem solvers, critical thinkers, and meaningful learners (Ahn, 2012, 7-8). Moreover, there is evidence that creativity-enhancing activities are facilitative of English-language learning in general, with studies showing "a positive effect for PABCL [personal -analogy-based creative lessons] on young learners' English language achievement whether they are high or low level" (Kang Nam Joon, 2017, 65-6)."

• **Social and Emotional Intelligence** Drama activities such as Reader's Theater offer an engaging way to integrate productive and receptive skills while also allowing students to connect emotion and cognition (Zyoud, 2010). As students read their parts with the emotion proper to the character and situation, they are given opportunities to know their own emotions and recognize them in others, and this helps develop their Social and Emotional intelligence (SEI), a term coined by noted psychologist Daniel Goleman that refers to the ability to recognize and manage emotions, deal with emotions and emotional situations appropriately and productively, and maintain and manage relationships (2005, 43). The Writing and Discussion Projects are intended to give students further opportunities to explore the social and ethical implications of the fable. The scripts contain themes such as Problem Solving and Advice, Bullies, Balancing Study and Rest, Peer Pressure, and Self-Esteem, and the questions and projects are all intended to help students make connections, personalize, and meaningfully explore the fables as they apply them to their own lives. In so doing, students develop the skills they need to become happy and well-functioning members of school and adult societies. SEI is also facilitative of academic success in general; Goleman explains that "helping children improve their self-awareness and confidence, manage their disturbing emotions and impulses, and increase their empathy pays off not just in improved behavior but in measurable academic achievement" (2005, xi).

• **Differentiated Instruction** Unlike in a role play, lower-level students can easily participate in a Reader's Theater performance and experience success. Little language production is required, but collaborative rehearsal can provide scaffolding, and roles can be assigned according to a student's level (See Appendix 1).

• **Multi-skill language development** Reader's Theater allows students to use all four language skills:

> **a. Reading** – readers are actively involved and read for the overall meaning, not just word by word. Teachers often approach a reading passage through "cold reading," wherein students are required to read sentences or sections aloud in turns. During such an exercise, students are not involved with the meaning of the text as a whole; rather, they are trying to predict which sentence will be "theirs" and making sure that they know how to pronounce all the words.
> Since they are focused on their own correct reading, they are not listening to the other readers. Cold Reading offers little fluency development and no chance

for personalization. Reader's Theater is collaborative and meaning-focused and allows for personalization and emotional engagement with the text as well as fluency development.

b. Listening – readers must listen actively to the other readers in order to read their lines at the right time; the audience is also engaged with the story and listens actively.

c. Speaking – readers can practice pronunciation and word and sentence stress and so become more comfortable with the sounds of English and gain fluency. Also, readers gain confidence in presentation skills. Readers are pushed to produce English during collaborative preparation, and this also greatly assists fluency development.

d. Writing – follow-up activities can include discussion or reflective journals on themes from the Reader's Theater Script. Students can also write or adapt their own scripts.

The Design of the Book

This book offers eight original Reader's Theater scripts, either written for this book or as models for my writing class, and including one script ("The Grasshopper and the Ants") that I adapted from a script written by three of my students. Each chapter is laid out as follows:

1) Pre-Script
i. Before Reading Questions
ii. Original Fable
iii. After Reading Questions

2) Reader's Theater
　i. Rehearsal and Reading Instructions
　ii. Reader's Theater Script (performance)

3) Post-Script (extension)
　i. After Performance Questions
　ii. Writing and Discussion Projects
　iii. Grammar and Vocabulary Focus

In the **Pre-Scrip**t section, the Before Reading Questions are intended to provide a meaningful learning set (schema activation) so that students are predisposed to read the original fable and relate it to their prior experience and knowledge. This, according to David Ausubel, will promote meaningful learning (Ausubel, 1967). The Original Fable and the After Reading Questions give the students a pre-understanding of the story and its lesson that will help them in understanding the Reader's Theater Script that follows.

The **Reader's Theater** section is intended to guide students as they collaborate to perform the script and to provide the benefits discussed above:

- collaborative work for motivation, scaffolding, and pushed output
- active reading for making input comprehensible, meaning and form focus, pronunciation practice, noticing of word and sentence stress, confidence and presentation skills
- reading with emotional engagement and understanding to help students develop social and emotional intelligence

The **Post-Script** section consists of After Performance Questions and Writing and Discussion Projects. This section is intended to provide meaningful, collaborative production opportunities and to help students think and reflect on the lesson of the fable and apply it to their own lives. Finally, each chapter concludes with a Grammar and Vocabulary Focus section that suggests grammatical features, vocabulary, and expressions that teachers can teach along with the Reader's Theater script, perhaps by helping them to notice lexical forms and their usage as recommended by the Lexical Approach.

Although each chapter can be taught as a complete lesson, teachers can also use the Reader's Theater script alone to supplement another lesson, such as a reading or grammar lesson. If teachers use the Writing and Discussion projects, they could either choose an appropriate project based on their students' level and interests or give their students some choices – choice is a great motivator and develops student autonomy (Dörnyei, 2010). Brief guidelines about rehearsal and performance precede each script. Appendix 1 (Performance Notes) contains more performance suggestions.

CHAPTER 1

BELLING THE CAT

CHAPTER

1

BELLING THE CAT

Before Reading

Share your answers to these questions in small groups.

1. What is one problem you have had in your life?

_____
_____

2. How did you solve the problem?

_____
_____

3. What can you do if you can't solve a problem by yourself?

_____
_____
_____

Belling the Cat

The mice lived in constant danger from the house cat. Since they were tired of being chased or eaten whenever they left their home inside the kitchen wall, they decided to have a meeting to find a solution to their problem. They discussed and rejected plan after plan. Eventually, a very young mouse rose up on his hind legs and made a proposal: "We can hang a bell around the cat's neck."

"What a great idea!" the other mice cried.

"Excellent suggestion!"

"Oh, yes! Then we would all know when the cat was near, so we could run away!"

They were accepting the proposal with great enthusiasm and applause until a quiet old mouse stood up to speak.

"This is indeed a very good suggestion and would probably solve our problems," he said. "Now, which one of us will put the bell around the cat's neck?"

Moral: It's easy to propose impossible solutions; it's harder to carry them out.

After Reading

1. What was the mice's problem?

_____

2. Why didn't the young mouse's proposal work?

_____

_____

Reader's Theater

In groups of five, first read through the script silently. [2]
Then identify the roles in the story and divide them among you.
Each reader should mark his or her lines by underlining or highlighting them.
Every reader should also mark the lines spoken by "All the Mice."

Read the script together a few times to practice. Ask your teacher about any words you don't know or can't pronounce. Be sure to read your lines at the right time. That means you have to listen carefully to the other readers. Also be sure to read your lines with the appropriate feeling or emotion for your character.

Belling the Cat

< Characters: Five Mice >

Scene 1

Mouse 1: Hey, have you guys seen Mickey?

Mouse 2: Didn't you hear the news?

Mouse 1: What news?

Mouse 2: Mickey is dead! The cat ate him!

Mouse 3: Yeah, he was just looking for food in the kitchen, and the cat jumped out and ate him.

Mouse 1: That's terrible. Poor Mickey!
We have to do something about that cat!

Mouse 4: Yeah! Let's have a meeting.

Mouse 3: Yeah! We have to do something about that lousy cat!

---

[2] Another option might be for the entire class to read the script chorally. With different groups being assigned different parts. Then each group could work on the script on their own, as is outlined above.

Scene 2

Mouse 1: Thank you all for coming to our meeting. We all agree that we have to do something about the cat.

All the Mice: Yeah! That's right! The cat! That lousy cat!

Mouse 1: Okay, who has a suggestion?

Mouse 5 (excitedly): We can shoot the cat!

Mouse 4: We don't have a gun.

Mouse 5: Oh.

Mouse 3: We can all sign a petition.

Mouse 4 (scornfully): A petition? What good would that do? The cat won't care about our petition!

Mouse 2: I know what we can do!

Mouse 3: What?

Mouse 2: We can put a bell around the cat's neck. Then we can hear the cat coming, and we can run away.

Mouse 4: That's a great idea!

All the Mice: Yeah! Great idea! You're a genius! Let's do it!

Scene 3

Mouse 1: Okay, we have all agreed to put a bell around the cat's neck. But we still need to decide one thing.

Mouse 5: What's that?

Mouse 1: Who will put the bell around the cat's neck?

All the Mice: Ahhh!

Mouse 1: Mouse 2, it was your idea.
   Will you put the bell around the cat's neck?

Mouse 2: Well, I'd like to, but I'm pretty busy today.
   In fact, I will be busy all week!

Mouse 1: How about you, Mouse 3?

Mouse 3: I don't feel well. I think I'm getting a cold. Achoo! Achoo!

Mouse 1: Will ANYONE put the bell around the cat's neck?

All the Mice: I'm busy! I'm sick! I have a date! My tail hurts! [3]

Mouse 1: Well, I guess it's easier to think of a plan than to do it.

All the Mice: Yeah! Talk is cheap!

- THE END -

---

[3] Rather than all the readers reading all the excuses together, this line might be more effective if different readers choose different excuses and then say them at the same time.

? After Performance Questions

1. What happened to Mickey?
   _____
   _____

2. Why couldn't the mice shoot the cat?
   _____
   _____

3. Can you think of a way to solve the mice's problem that would really work?
   _____
   _____
   _____
   _____

Writing & Discussion Projects

1. Retell the story so the mice succeed in putting a bell around the cat's neck.

2. Best Advice Game

   A. Go over some patterns that students can use to give advice:

You can	You can get up earlier.
You should	You should get up earlier.
Why don't you	Why don't you get up earlier?
Have you tried	Have you tried getting up earlier?

Help them to notice that the first three are followed by the base form of a verb while the last one is followed by a gerund (-ing form).

   B. Divide the class into groups of four or five.

   C. Each group gets a set of 12 problem cards
      (I am always late for school. I had a fight with my sister because she read my Kakao Talk messages ... etc.)

I am always late for school.

I have two close friends who hate each other.

I become nervous when I am not with my cellphone.

I sometimes feel like I am a bad person.

My parents want me to be good at everything, but I don't want to be a superman or superwoman.

I get angry very often. How can I control my temper?

I don't want to do anything. I am just so bored all the time.

I want to have a pet, but I have an allergy to animal hair.

I have never won any arm-wrestling game. How can I be strong enough?

I think I'm way too busy with studying and all these Hagwon.

I have a friend who is too loud in public places. I am often embarrassed.

I want to be close to this girl/boy, but I am too shy.

D. Each group places the cards face down on the table.

E. A student draws a card and reads it. Each other group member gives advice. The card goes to the student who gave the best advice.

F. The student to the right of the first student draws a card and reads it. The others give advice and the student who gave the best advice gets the card. The student with the most cards at the end wins.

G. The students share their best pieces of advice with the whole class.

 Grammar & Vocabulary Focus

* Grammar

1. Agree To vs. Agree With

> "Agree with" is only used with nouns. "Agree to" is used with verbs or with certain nouns, like "compromise" or "settlement," that are the result of negotiation.

You "agree with" a person or a person's idea or opinion.
- I agree with my friend that *Black Panther* is a great movie.
- I agree with his opinion.
- Someone once said, "Love is the only rational act." I agree with that statement.

You "agree to" a course of action (verb) or to the result of a course of action (noun).
- I agreed to study hard next semester.
- The National Assembly agreed to compromise (verb).
- The National Assembly agreed to a compromise (noun).

> Teachers can help students find examples of "agree to" in the script.

2. Can (and other modals) plus base form of verb

> The teacher can help students to find examples of "can + base form of verb" in the script.
> The Best Advice Game also practices this form.

* Vocabulary

Lousy

an insulting adjective used in informal speech

It implies that the person or other noun it modifies is useless, bad, no good, dirty, etc. *("Lousy" literally means that the person it describes has body lice.)*

Petition

a document that collects signatures in support of a certain cause

For instance, people might want a drug company to reduce the price of a life-saving drug so that sick people can afford it. When enough signatures have been gathered, the petition is presented to the drug company CEO, ideally with a lot of press coverage.

* Expressions/idioms

"You're a genius!"

Use this expression when someone has an idea or suggestion that you strongly approve of.

"I'm getting a cold."

"I am becoming sick with a cold." You can also say, "I'm catching a cold. I caught a cold. I have a cold."

"Talk is cheap!"

Use this expression when someone proposes to do something or makes a promise but really will never do it.

CHAPTER

THE SHEPHERD BOY AND THE WOLF

CHAPTER

2

THE SHEPHERD BOY AND THE WOLF

 **Before Reading**
Share your answers to these questions in small groups.

1. Have you ever played a trick on someone as a joke? What did you do?
   _____
   _____

2. Has someone ever played a trick on you or on one of your friends? What did they do? How did you or your friend feel?
   _____
   _____
   _____

The Shepherd Boy and the Wolf

A Shepherd Boy was tending his flock of sheep near a village and thought it would be fun to trick the villagers by pretending that a wolf was attacking the sheep. He shouted, "Wolf! Wolf!" and when the people came running he laughed at them.

He did this more than once. At last a wolf really did come, and the boy cried, "Wolf! Wolf!" as loud as he could, but the people but the people were so used to his cries for help that they paid no attention to him, and the wolf was free to eat as many sheep as it wanted.

 **After Reading**

1. How did the boy trick the villagers?

_____

2. Why didn't the villagers come when the boy saw a real wolf?

_____

_____

 **Reader's Theater**

In groups of five, first read through the script silently.
Then identify the roles in the story and divide them among you.
Each reader should mark his or her lines by underlining or highlighting them.

Read the script together a few times to practice. Ask your teacher about any words you don't know or can't pronounce. Be sure to read your lines at the right time. That means you have to listen carefully to the other readers. Also be sure to read your lines with the appropriate feeling or emotion for your character.
Even though the wolf only growls, this is an important part of the story.
Be sure to growl in a scary way.

The Shepherd Boy & the Wolf

< Characters: A Shepherd Boy, Three Farmers, a Wolf >

Scene 1

Shepherd Boy: Well, here I am again, in the same old meadow, watching the same old sheep! How boring! Nothing ever happens! The birds sing, the sheep eat grass, the sun shines, the clouds float in the sky, and the forest just stands there at the edge of the meadow. Every day is exactly the same! I'm so bored! This job is so boring! I wish something exciting would happen! Maybe a wolf will come out of the forest, a huge wolf with sharp teeth, a long red tongue, and cruel grey eyes!
Hey! I know! I'll play a trick on those farmers over in the next field. They can't see me from there . . . HELP! WOLF! WOLF!

Scene 2

Farmer 1: Hey, did you hear that?

Farmer 2: Yes! The shepherd boy saw a wolf!

Farmer 3: A wolf! Let's go! Bring that pitchfork!

Farmer 1: Let's go! *(The farmers run to the meadow)* [4]

Scene 3

Farmer 1 (out of breath): We're here!

Farmer 2: Where's the wolf?

Farmer 1: Yes, where is it?

Shepherd Boy (laughing)**:** There isn't any wolf!

Farmer 2: No wolf?

Shepherd Boy: You guys sure ran fast! You're lucky you didn't fall down and hurt yourselves! Ha! Ha! Ha! Ha!

Farmer 3: What a dirty trick! There wasn't any wolf!

Farmer 1: That boy made us look like fools!

Shepherd Boy: Can't you guys take a joke?

Farmer 2: Come on, fellas, let's get back to work. *(The farmers go back to their field)*

Scene 4

Shepherd Boy: Boy, that was fun! Those farmers looked so silly! They were really scared! One farmer almost tripped over his pitchfork! Ha! Ha! Ha! . . . Hey, what was that? I thought I heard a noise at the edge of the forest . . . Did I hear a wolf growl?

---

4   The readers can briefly run in place.

Wolf (growling): Grrrrrr!

Shepherd Boy: Oh, no! It IS a wolf! A huge wolf with sharp teeth, a long red tongue, and cruel grey eyes! HELP! WOLF! WOLF!

Scene 5

Farmer 1: It's that boy again!

Farmer 2: Does he think we're stupid?

Farmer 3: He can't fool US again!

Farmer 1: Just ignore him.
He'll soon get bored with his silly game and stop yelling.

Scene 6

Shepherd Boy: HELP! WOLF! A REAL WOLF! HELP! FARMERS! HELP ME!

Wolf: Grrrrrr! *(The wolf drags the boy into the forest and eats him)*

Scene 7

Farmer 1 (after a pause): See! I told you he'd get bored and stop!

- THE END -

After Performance Questions

1. Why did the boy pretend to see a wolf?

_____

_____

2. How did the farmers feel after the boy had tricked them?

_____

_____

 **Writing & Discussion Projects**

1. Retell the story so that the boy escapes from the wolf.

2. Write a script about the trial of the boy (who wasn't eaten) for being neglectful and allowing the wolf to eat the sheep.

3. Choose one of the tricks you discussed in "Before Reading" and write a short RT script about it.

4. **Write a letter from one of the farmers explaining to the village council how the shepherd boy came to be eaten by a wolf.**

Dear Honorable Village Council Members,

_____

_____

_____

_____

_____

_____

_____

_____

Sincerely, _____

Grammar & Vocabulary Focus

* Grammar

Present participles and past participles have different meanings.
Teachers can help their students find examples in the script.

Use the present participle when you talk about a <u>cause</u>:

- The movie was exciting. (It caused us to feel excited.)
- The lecture was boring. (It caused us to feel bored.)
- Studying English is tiring. (It causes us to feel tired.)

Use the past participle when you talk about an <u>effect</u>:

- The movie was exciting, so the audience was excited.
- The lecture was boring, so the audience was bored.
- Studying English is tiring, so it makes us tired.

Cause	Effect
exciting, boring, interesting, etc.	excited, bored, interested, etc.
With some verbs, the "cause" word is NOT the present participle.	
scary	scared
impressive	impressed
outrageous	outraged
burdensome	burdened
bothersome (bothering)	bothered
troublesome (troubling)	troubled
worrisome (offensive)	worried
offensive (offending)	offended

* Vocabulary

Pitchfork
a farming tool used for stacking hay

"To play a trick on someone"
to deceive someone or cause him or her to feel foolish or embarrassed in order to laugh at him or her. You can also say, "Play a joke on someone."

"To trip over something"
to fall because some object or obstacle causes you to lose your balance

* Expressions/idioms

"Can't you guys take a joke?"
Use this expression when the person you have played a trick on becomes angry. Often people who play jokes on others become angry when jokes are played on them. In that case, you can tell the person.
"You can dish it out but you can't take it."

"A dose of your own medicine"
You can use this expression when you play a trick on someone who played a trick on you: "I'm giving you a dose of your own medicine."
or "Here's a dose of your own medicine."

CHAPTER

THE WIND AND THE SUN

CHAPTER

3

THE WIND AND THE SUN

Before Reading

Share your answers to these questions in small groups.

1. **Has someone ever forced you to do something that you didn't want to do? How did you feel?**

   _____
   _____

2. **If you wanted something from your parents or from a friend, what strategy could you use to get it?**

   _____
   _____
   _____

The Wind and the Sun

On a bright, chilly day in April, the Wind was showing off in the sky.

"Watch what I can do to that tree," he shouted. He blew strongly, and the tree creaked [5] and groaned and bent down towards the ground.

"See?" boasted the Wind. "That tree is bowing to me. I'm the strongest in the sky!"

"Don't be so sure," said the Sun. "I think I'm stronger than you."

"No way!" shouted the Wind.

They kept arguing, and finally they agreed to have a test of strength.

"Here comes a traveler. Let us see who can strip him of his coat," [6] said the Sun.

"That will be easy!" said the Wind. "He cannot resist my mighty power!"

The Wind blew as hard as he could. But the traveler just wrapped his coat more tightly around himself.

Then it was the Sun's turn. At first he shone very gently. When the traveler felt the sun's warmth, he unbuttoned his coat. The sun went on shining brighter and brighter. "What funny weather!" said the traveler. "First it was windy and cold, but now it's hot!" Before long he took off his coat and put it in his backpack.

"You lost, Wind," said the Sun. "Now you can see that persuasion is better than force."

After Reading

1. What did the traveler do when the wind blew?

_____

2. If the North Wind was a person, what kind of person would he/she be?

_____

3. If the sun was a person, what kind of person would he/she be?

_____

5 creaked" – made the sound that wood makes when it is under stress
6 strip him of his coat" – take his coat off

Aesop's Fables often use characters like the Wind and the Sun to represent certain types of people. They also use animal characters.[7]

What animal or other type of character would you use to represent the following kinds of people?

A greedy person _____

A tricky person _____

A bully _____

A kind person _____

A person who is often afraid _____

A brave person _____

A lazy person _____

Compare your answers with your partner's.

Imagine that you are these different things in the sky. Imagine how each one might feel. Then imagine why each one might feel like that. Complete the sentences.

If I were the wind, I would feel _____ because _____.

If I were the snow, I would feel _____ because _____.

If I were the sun, I would feel _____ because _____.

If I were a cloud, I would feel _____ because _____.

If I were the rain, I would feel _____ because _____.

If I were the moon, I would feel _____ because _____.

Compare your answers with your partner's.

---

[7] All the characters are male in this script, but the script would work just as well if they were female. If the readers want to change the gender of any characters, they should go through their part and change the pronouns: he>>she; his>>her, etc. This also applies to characters in other scripts.

Reader's Theater

In groups of four, first read through the script silently. Then identify the roles in the story and divide them among you. Each reader should mark his or her lines by underlining or highlighting them.

Read the script together a few times to practice. Ask your teacher about any words you don't know or can't pronounce. Be sure to read your lines at the right time. That means you have to listen carefully to the other readers. Also be sure to read your lines with the appropriate feeling or emotion for your character.

The Wind & the Sun
< Characters: Narrator, Wind, Sun, Traveler >

Scene 1

Narrator: On a bright, chilly day in April, the Wind was showing off in the sky. He started by blowing the clouds around, but that was too easy. Then he noticed an ancient oak tree standing in a field.

Wind: Hey, you clouds! Watch what I can do to that big tree down there!

Narrator: The wind puffed out his cheeks and blew strongly. The old tree creaked and groaned and bent down towards the ground. It bent so low that its leaves almost brushed the grass.

Wind: See? That tree is bowing to me! I'm the strongest in the sky!

Sun: Don't be so sure. I think I'm stronger than you.

Wind: Don't make me laugh, Sun! I can easily beat you! Who makes tornadoes? Who makes hurricanes? I do! I can destroy trees and buildings! I can sink ships at sea! Nothing is too hard for me!

Sun: I still think I'm stronger than you. Look! Here comes a traveler. Let's see who can be the first to strip him of his coat. The one who strips the coat off first is the strongest in the sky!

Wind: Are you kidding? That will be easy! He cannot resist my mighty power!

Scene 2

Narrator: The Wind blew as hard as he could. But the traveler just wrapped his coat more tightly around himself.

Traveler: Good heavens! What kind of wind is this? I can hardly stand! I'd better hold on to my coat!

Narrator: Then it was the Sun's turn. At first he shone very gently. When the traveler felt the sun's warmth, he unbuttoned his coat. The sun went on shining brighter and brighter.

Sun: Bling! Bling! Bling!

Traveler: What funny weather! First it was windy and cold, but now it's as hot as August! It must be global warming.

Narrator: The sun kept shining, and before long the traveler took off his coat and put it in his backpack.

Sun: You lost, Wind! Now you see that persuasion is better than force.

- THE END -

After Performance Questions

1. Who had a contest?

2. Who won the contest?

3. Why did he/she win?

4. What kind of person is the wind?

5. How can you tell?

6. What kind of person is the sun?

7. How can you tell?

Writing & Discussion Projects

1. If you want something from your parents or from a friend, what strategy can you use?

2. Is persuasion always better than force? Think of a situation where the wind's way is better. Retell the story so that the Wind wins.

3. Retell the story of the Wind and the Sun in a school setting. Who could be the Wind and the Sun? What could the contest be about?

4. Write an email from the traveler to his friend describing his journey.

To : _____   Date : _____
Cc : _____
Bcc : _____
Subject : _____

Hi _____ ,

_____
_____
_____
_____
_____
_____
_____
_____
_____

Best,

_____

 **Grammar & Vocabulary Focus**

* Grammar

1. Students sometimes produce incorrect sentences like these:

- They are easy to learn English.
- They are hard to learn English.

The phrase "easy to learn" can only have "it" as a pronoun subject, because we cannot "learn" a person, only a skill or body of knowledge.[8]

Examples :
- English is easy for them to learn.
- They learn English easily.

The phrase "hard to learn" can only have "it" as a pronoun subject, because we cannot "learn" a person, only a skill or body of knowledge.

However, the adverb "hardly" means "barely," so we cannot use it as we used "easily" in the second example sentence above. Instead, we must use "with difficulty" or "with effort," etc.

Examples :
- English is hard for them to learn.
- They are learning English with difficulty.

> Teachers can help their students find examples of "easy/easily" and "hard" in the script.
> "Hardly" is also there, meaning "barely."

---

[8] "Easy to Learn" and "Hard to Learn" sometimes also have "they" as a pronoun subject :
"I like Asian Languages. They are easy to learn."

2. Comparative/superlative

With one-syllable words, we form the comparative by adding the suffix er to the adjective: strong – stronger; big – bigger; easy – easier.

With multi-syllable words, we don't change the adjective and use "more": tightly – more tightly; beautiful – more beautiful.

We form the superlative by adding the suffix –est to the adjective: strong – the strongest; big – the biggest; easy – the easiest.

With multi-syllable words, we don't change the adjective and use "most": beautiful – the most beautiful.

We need to use the article "the" with superlatives because the noun is specific; only one character is "the strongest in the sky."

The adjective "good" is irregular: good, better, the best.

> Teachers can help their students find examples of comparative and superlative adjectives in the script.

3. Word families

Students might find it helpful to notice and learn word families:

strong, strongly, stronger, the strongest, strength, strengthen
easy, easily, easier, easiest, ease (noun and verb)

* Vocabulary

To creak
to make a sound like wood under stress: "The floorboards creaked as we walked through the old house."

To groan
to make a sound of pain

Tornado
a violent windstorm with a destructive funnel-shaped cloud

Hurricane
a large, powerful storm, similar to a typhoon

* Expressions/idioms

To strip him of his coat
to remove his coat from him

To show off
to act in a way that draws attention to oneself or one's abilities

CHAPTER

THE RABBIT AND THE TURTLE

CHAPTER

4

THE RABBIT AND THE TURTLE

 **Before Reading**
Share your answers to these questions in small groups.

1. Have you ever heard the saying "slow and steady wins the race"? Explain what it means in your own words

   _____
   _____

2. Can you think of any Korean proverbs that mean "slow and steady wins the race"? What are they?

   _____
   _____
   _____

The Rabbit and the Turtle

One sunny day in the park, a rabbit was teasing a turtle for being so slow. "Look at me," the rabbit said. "I can run rings around a slow thing like you!"

He ran in circles around the turtle, laughing and jumping.

Finally the turtle had had enough. "Stop showing off," she said. "I'll race you, and I'll bet I win!" The rabbit was very amused at this idea, but he agreed. "I'll show that stupid turtle not to challenge me!" he thought. They agreed that the fox would set the course for them and be the judge.

When the fox said, "Ready, set, go!" they both started together, but the rabbit was soon so far ahead of the turtle that he couldn't see her when he looked back.

"I can afford to take a break," he thought. He stopped to rest under a shady tree and almost immediately fell fast asleep.

Meanwhile the turtle kept plodding [9] on, and after a while she had almost reached the finish line. The rabbit woke up with a start, [10] saw that the turtle was about to win, and ran as fast as he could. He ran like greased lightning, [11] but he was too late; the turtle crossed the finish line first.

Moral: Slow and steady wins the race.

After Reading

1. Why did the turtle challenge the rabbit to a race?

_____

2. What does "like greased lightning" mean?

_____

9   Plodding – walking slowly and deliberately
10 With a start – suddenly and with a jerk, as someone wakes up who has fallen asleep on the subway
11 Like greased lightning – a folk expression that means "very fast." Lightening is fast, and the imaginary lubrication on it makes it even faster.

Reader's Theater

In groups of five, first read through the script silently. Then identify the roles in the story and divide them among you. Each reader should mark his or her lines by underlining or highlighting them.

Read the script together a few times to practice. Ask your teacher about any words you don't know or can't pronounce. Be sure to read your lines at the right time. That means you have to listen carefully to the other readers. Also be sure to read your lines with the appropriate feeling or emotion for your character.

The Rabbit and the Turtle

< Characters: Rabbit, Turtle, Squirrel, Magpie, Mrs. Hedgehog >

Scene 1

Rabbit (running and jumping): Nobody is faster than me!
I'm the fastest animal in the Park! I'm faster than the squirrels! I'm faster than the chipmunks! I'm faster than the cats and the dogs!
And I'm certainly faster than YOU, Turtle!

Turtle: Maybe you are and maybe you're not.

Rabbit (standing still): Maybe I'm NOT? Are you crazy?
I can run around the park twice before you take one step!

Turtle: Maybe you can, and maybe you can't.

Rabbit: Hey, Squirrel! Did you hear that? The turtle says he's faster than me!

Turtle: I said MAYBE I'm faster.

Rabbit: Whatever! Hey, Mrs. Hedgehog!
The turtle says he's the fastest animal in the park!

Turtle: No, I didn't. I said I was faster than YOU. Maybe.

Rabbit: Whatever! I'll bet you a week's worth of strawberries that I can beat you in a race.

Squirrel: Go on, Turtle! Race him!

Turtle: Well, okay. Where do we race to?

Rabbit: Let's race from the Park to the Subway Station and back. That will be a good warm-up exercise for a great runner like me.

Squirrel: We must have a fair race.
A week's worth of strawberries is a big prize! Magpie, will you fly down to the Subway Station? Make sure that both of them touch the half-way point. Mrs. Hedgehog and I will stay here at the finish line.

Magpie: Okay, I'll do it.

Mrs. Hedgehog: Okay, I'll wait with you.
But I need to get back to my babies soon. Have you seen them? They're the most beautiful babies in the park!

Rabbit: Don't worry, Mrs. Hedgehog. It won't take long.

Squirrel: Great! Here's the starting line.
The one that gets back first is the winner. Are you both ready?

Rabbit and Turtle: Yes! I'm ready!

Squirrel: Okay, then – ready . . . set . . . GO!

Magpie: Wow! That rabbit took off like a rocket!
I can't even see him anymore! I'd better fly down to the Subway Station before he gets there!

Scene 2

Turtle: Right foot, left foot, steady and slow. I'll be back before you know!

Rabbit: Here I am at the Subway Station! Hey, Magpie, I'm here! Whew! This is too easy! I'll be back before that stupid turtle reaches the Coffee Shop!

Turtle: Front leg, back leg, slow and steady!

Rabbit: Whew! I'm halfway back to the park already!
Let me catch my breath . . .
Hey, there's a PC Room! I've got plenty of time. That turtle is such a joke! I'll go in and play a few computer games!

Turtle: Right foot, left foot, steady and slow. I'll be back before you know!

Rabbit: Hey, they have my favorite – World of Rabbitcraft! Let's play!

Turtle: Front leg, back leg, slow and steady!

Rabbit: I'm at level three already! Let's keep playing!

Turtle: Right foot, left foot, steady and slow. I'll be back before you know!

Rabbit: Level five! I'm playing better than I ever have!

Turtle: Front leg, back leg, slow and steady!

Rabbit: Wow! I'm at level six already! Level seven, here I come!

Turtle: Right foot, left foot, celebration! Here I am at the Subway Station!

Magpie: Finally! Here's the turtle! Now I can fly back to the park.

Rabbit: Level seven! My skills are awesome! My avatar is unbeatable!

Turtle: Right foot, left foot, steady and slow. I'll be back before you know!

Scene 3

Squirrel: Hey, Magpie? Have you seen that rabbit? We've been waiting almost three hours!

Magpie: The rabbit reached the Station about two hours ago, and the turtle showed up about an hour after that. Then I flew back here.

Squirrel: Well, fly down there again and see if you can see them. I'm getting hungry. I need to find some nuts!

Mrs. Hedgehog: And I have to get back to my pretty babies!

Magpie: Okay! . . . I didn't see the rabbit, but the turtle is almost at the Coffee Shop on her way back!

Squirrel: Wow! Where is the rabbit?

Scene 4

Rabbit: Level twelve! My all-time high score! Let's see what happens at level thirteen! Go get 'em, Rabbit Warrior!

Turtle: Right foot, left foot, steady and slow. I'll be back before you know!

Squirrel: Hey, here's the turtle! He's only a few meters from the finish line!

Magpie: Where's the rabbit? I don't see him anywhere.

Rabbit: Level fifteen! I didn't know this game had so many levels!
   Wait . . . what time is it? How long have I been here? Oh, no! I forgot about the race!

Scene 5

Turtle: Right foot, left foot, steady and slow. I'll be back before you know!

Squirrel: Come on, Turtle! You're almost there!

Magpie: Here comes the rabbit, like a streak of greased lightning!

Turtle: Front leg, back leg, slow and steady!
   I've come back to the Park already!

Squirrel, Magpie, and Mrs. Hedgehog: The turtle wins!

Rabbit (out of breath): Here I am! Where's the turtle? Where's the turtle?

Squirrel, Magpie, and Mrs. Hedgehog: You lost! The turtle won!

Rabbit: Hey, wait a minute . . .

Squirrel: You owe the turtle a week's worth of strawberries.
   You'll have to get some from the "Grandmother Mart" every day!

Magpie: For a week!

Rabbit: Okay, okay! I'll use my Olympic prize money!

Turtle: Now I'll relax and stuff my face . . .

All: Slow and steady wins the race!

- THE END -

❓ After Performance Questions

1. What prize did the turtle win?
   _____
   _____

2. How many levels did the rabbit complete in World of Rabbitcraft?
   _____
   _____

3. Why did the turtle win?
   _____
   _____

 ## Writing & Discussion Projects

1. Why did the turtle agree to race the rabbit? Did the turtle really think he/she could win?

2. Retell the story in a school setting. What could the race or contest be about? Who could be the rabbit? Who could be the turtle?

 **Grammar & Vocabulary Focus**

* Grammar (advanced)

1. "That" clauses

The pronoun "that" is often used as a relative pronoun in a dependent clause.

• **"That"** complements: I didn't know that this game had so many levels!
In sentences like these, **"that"** is often left out: I didn't know this game had so many levels.

• Restrictive relative clauses: The one that gets back first is the winner.
In sentences like these, **"that"** is NEVER left out.
("The one who gets back first is the winner" is also correct.)

• Indirect discourse: The turtle says that he's faster than me.
In sentences like these, **"that"** is often left out: The turtle says he's faster than me.

"That" is also used as a demonstrative determiner: "**that** stupid turtle."

> Teachers can help their students find examples of "that" clauses in the script. More advanced students can identify them as complements, restrictive clauses, or indirect discourse. They may need help because "that" is often left out.

2. Comparative/superlative (see Chapter 3)

> Teachers can help their students find examples of comparative and superlative adjectives in the script.

* Vocabulary

Hedgehog
고슴도치 (a small prickly animal with a sharp nose)

Squirrel
다람쥐 (a small animal with a fluffy tail that eats nuts)

Magpie
까치 (a black and white bird with a noisy voice)

Avatar
in gaming, the on-screen character that represents the player

* Expressions/idioms

Like a rocket – very fast

Like greased lightning – very fast

Note: We can compare one thing with another thing using "like" or "as." With nouns we use "like" and with adjectives, adverbs, and verbs we use "as." Many English expressions have these comparisons:

- Time flies like an arrow.
- Usain Bolt is as fast as lightning.
- Jack eats like a pig (a messy eater)

Sally eats like a bird (a person who doesn't eat much); No one skates as well as Kim Yuna, etc.

A week's worth of strawberries

This expression means "Enough strawberries to last one week." We can change the item and the length of time: "A day's worth of rice." We can also use " supply" instead of "worth": "A month's supply of ice cream bars." This means the same thing as "Enough ice cream bars to last one month." Of course, when you say that, you have to know how many ice cream bars you usually eat in a day.

CHAPTER

5

THE LION AND THE MOUSE

CHAPTER

5

THE LION AND THE MOUSE

 **Before Reading**

Share your answers to these questions in small groups.

1. What do you think this expression means: "Even a mouse can help a lion"?

_____
_____

2. Have you ever done a big favor for someone? What did you do?

_____
_____
_____

The Lion and the Mouse

Once a Mouse woke up a sleeping Lion by running over his face. Losing his temper [12], the Lion grabbed the Mouse and was about to kill it. The Mouse, terrified, pleaded with the Lion to spare its life. "Please let me go," it cried, "and one day I will repay you for your kindness." This made the Lion laugh, so he let the Mouse go.

One day, the Lion got entangled in a net that had been left by some hunters. The Mouse heard the Lion's angry roars and ran to the place where the Lion was trapped. Immediately it started gnawing [13] and chewing the ropes with its tiny sharp teeth, and soon the Lion was free. "There," said the Mouse. "You laughed at me, but now you see that even a Mouse can help a Lion."

After Reading

1. Why was the Lion angry?

_____

2. Why did the Lion laugh at the Mouse?

_____

_____

[12] "Losing his temper" – getting angry, becoming angry
[13] Gnawing (pronounced "nawing") – chewing (this verb is usually used for small animals)

 **Reader's Theater**

In groups of seven, first read through the script silently. Then identify the roles in the story and divide them among you. Each reader should mark his or her lines by underlining or highlighting them.

Read the script together a few times to practice. Ask your teacher about any words you don't know or can't pronounce. Be sure to read your lines at the right time. That means you have to listen carefully to the other readers. Also be sure to read your lines with the appropriate feeling or emotion for your character.

The Lion and the Mouse

< Characters: Lion, Mouse, Mouse's Wife, Hunter 1, Hunter 2, Buffalo, Cheetah >

Scene 1

Mouse: I'm going out to look for food.

Mouse's Wife: Be careful! The jungle is dangerous for little creatures like us.

Mouse: Don't worry! I'm always careful.

Scene 2

Mouse: Now where can I find some food? Oh, look! There's a big yellow mountain! Let's climb over it! How strange! This mountain is covered with fur!

Lion (waking up): Who disturbed my sweet sleep? Is it a mosquito? Ah, got you! It's not a mosquito. It's a little mouse!

Mouse: Please, King Lion! Let me go! I didn't mean to wake you up.

Lion: And why should I let you go? You have disturbed the rest of the King! As punishment I shall eat you up!

Mouse: Please don't eat me! I have a wife and children at home.
If I don't find food for them, they will starve to death.

Lion: I don't care! If they are hungry, they can beg for food.

Mouse: Please, King Lion! If you let me go, I will repay you some day!

Lion (laughing): Ha, ha, ha! How could a little mouse help a mighty lion?

Mouse: I don't know, but I promise I will help you!

Lion: Well, you made me laugh, and it's time for me to get up anyway.
I'll let you go this time. But if you disturb me again,
I will eat you without mercy!

Mouse: Oh, thank you, Your Majesty! Thank you, thank you, thank you!

Scene 3

Hunter 1: This looks like a good place for our net.
I can tell from the signs that lions come here often. If we catch a lion,
we can sell it for a good price!

Hunter 2: Yes, the circus will pay us a lot of money if we catch a lion!

Hunter 1: I've heard that rich Americans pay even more.
They want the heads of wild animals as trophies. They hang them on the
walls of their mansions to impress their guests.

Hunter 2: Ok, the net is in place. We've hidden it so well that it's almost
invisible. Let's go check our other traps.
We can come back later to see if we caught anything.

Scene 4

Lion: Now I'm getting hungry. Maybe I should have eaten that little mouse. Never mind! If I had eaten the mouse, he would only have been a tiny mouthful. I need a big meal. I'll go find my girlfriends. Those lionesses catch big animals all the time. Ow! What this? Vines? Spider webs? No, ropes! I'm trapped in a net! I can't break free! The ropes are too strong and thick! Help! Somebody help me!

Mrs. Buffalo: What's all that noise? Who is yelling?

Lion: Help! Help!

Mrs. Buffalo: It's King Lion! He's trapped in a net!

Lion: Mrs. Buffalo, help me!

Mrs. Buffalo: Why should I help you? You ate my baby last year. I hope they sell you to the circus!

Lion: If these ropes were a little weaker, I could break free . . . Uggh! . . . It's no use! I'm trapped! If they sell me to a circus, I'll have to do tricks! They'll whip me and make me live in a tiny cage! What a disgrace! Help! Help!

Mrs. Cheetah: Lion! What are you doing?

Lion: Mrs. Cheetah! I'm trapped! Please help me! If you were trapped, you know that I would help you!

Mrs. Cheetah: I know no such thing! As a matter of fact, I remember how you chased me away from the antelope that I killed last week. I was going to feed it to my cubs, but you stole it and ate it! Because of you, one of my cubs starved to death!

Lion: I'm sorry! Please help me!

Cheetah: Forget it! I hope the hunters cut your head off and sell it to a rich American so he can put it on his wall!

Scene 5

Lion: Help! Help! Won't anyone help me?

Mouse: What's that? Do I hear something?

Lion: Help! Help!

Mouse's Wife: It sounds like some big animal yelling for help.

Lion: Help! Help!

Mouse: It's the lion! Now's my chance to repay the debt!

Mouse's Wife: Don't go, honey! It could be dangerous.

Mouse: I've got to go. The lion is my friend. I owe him.

Mouse's Wife: Then I'm going with you. You may need my help.

Mouse: Here we are. The lion's all wrapped up in something. King Lion, what happened?

Lion: I got caught in a net! I can't break these thick ropes.

Mouse: Ropes? No problem! Mice are born to gnaw through ropes!

Lion: Hurry! The hunters could be back at any minute! If they catch me, they'll sell me to a zoo or a circus! Or maybe they'll cut off my head so some rich American can put it on his wall.

Mouse: We're chewing as fast as we can! . . . (Chewing sounds) . . . There! You're free!

Lion: I'm free! Thank you, Mouse! I was wrong to doubt you. And thank you, too, Mrs. Mouse.

Mrs. Mouse: You're welcome, Your Majesty. Isn't my husband awesome?

Mouse: See? Even a mouse can help a lion!

- THE END -

 **After Performance Questions**

1. Why did the hunters want to catch a Lion?
   _____
   _____

2. Who would pay more than a zoo if the hunters sold the Lion?
   _____
   _____

3. Why didn't the buffalo help the lion?
   _____
   _____

4. How does the Mouse's wife feel about her husband?
   _____
   _____

5. How can you tell that she feels that way?
   _____
   _____

Writing & Discussion Projects

1. Retell the story in a school or business setting. Who could be the Mouse? Who could be the Lion? How could the Mouse help the Lion?

2. Here is an imaginary story: First, imagine that you are all grown up. Next, imagine that you are in your own neighborhood when two foreigners ask you for directions to a certain restaurant. The foreigners are an old couple, and they seem very nice. You know where the restaurant is, but the location is very hard to find, so you lead them to the restaurant.[14] The whole journey takes about five minutes. The old couple is very grateful, and wants to give you ₩50,000 as a thank-you gift. What do you do? Why? Can you also think of a reason to do the thing that you chose NOT to do?

_____
_____
_____
_____
_____
_____

[14] The teacher should warn students that they need to be very careful around strangers and should never go places with them.

 Grammar & Vocabulary Focus

* Grammar (advanced)

"If" clauses with "will" and would"

It is important to distinguish between conditional statements that state factual implications (will) and those that state hypothetical situations (would).

"Will" is used in statements expressing factual implications or predictions. The verb in the "if" clause is in the present tense. (This is called "the first conditional.")

- If I drink five bottles of cider, I will feel sick.
- If it rains, the picnic will be cancelled.

(These sentences are predicting what will happen if the "if" clauses are fulfilled.)

"Would" is used in hypothetical statements. The verb in the "if" clause is in the past tense. (This is called "the second conditional.")

- If cider didn't taste sweet, people wouldn't drink it.
- If I won the lottery, I would buy my parents a house.

(Cider does taste sweet; I haven't won the lottery. The "if" clauses are untrue, hypothetical statements.)

> Teachers can help their students find examples of "if" clauses in the script. There are many examples of clauses that use "will." There is one example of a clause that uses "would." There is also one example of a clause that uses "would have." This is called the "third conditional." See the table after the Vocabulary/Expressions section.

* Vocabulary

Mosquito
모기 (a small biting insect that bothers people in the summer)

Trophy
something that you get as a prize for winning

Invisible
something that cannot be seen is invisible

Buffalo
물소 (a large grass-eating animal found in Africa)

Cheetah
치타 (a large meat-eating African member of the cat family)

* Expressions/idioms

"Mice were born to gnaw through ropes"
Mice chew through ropes very well.

To repay a debt
to do something helpful for someone who has helped you; to return the money that you borrowed from someone

to doubt someone
(1) to believe that someone cannot do something;
(2) to believe that someone is not telling the truth

I owe him
I am indebted to him; I owe him a favor.

Forget it!
(1) a way of saying, "No!"
(2) a way of saying "You're welcome!"

"I know no such thing!"
Say this when someone says, for example, "I'm the best student in the class," and you want to strongly deny that the statement is true.

"If clauses" or conditionals.

If clauses (conditionals) describe what might happen (in the present or future) or what might have happened (in the past). There are four types of conditionals.

The zero conditional

This conditional makes a general statement about something which always happens. It uses two simple present tense verbs.

- If students don't study, they usually don't get a good grade.
- If a car has no gasoline, it doesn't start.

The first conditional

This conditional describes things that could easily come true in the future, things which we can confidently predict. It uses the simple present and the future with "will."

- If I drink five bottles of soju, I will get drunk.
- I can't swim. If I fall into the water, I will drown.

The second conditional

This conditional describes things in the present or future that are probably not going to happen. It uses simple past and "would."

- If soju didn't have any alcohol, people wouldn't drink it.
- If I won the lottery, I would buy a house for my parents.

The third conditional

This conditional describes things in the past that didn't happen. It imagines what might have happened. It uses the past perfect and "would have."

- If I had studied harder, I would have passed the test.
- If I hadn't eaten that second pizza, I wouldn't feel so sick right now.

CHAPTER

6

THE MAN, THE BOY, AND THE DONKEY

CHAPTER

6

THE MAN, THE BOY, AND THE DONKEY

 **Before Reading**
Share your answers to these questions in small groups.

1. Explain this proverb in your own words:
   "Try to please everyone and you will please no one."
   _____
   _____

2. A group of your friends are smoking cigarettes after school. They urge you to smoke one with them, but you know that cigarettes are very bad for your health. How do you answer them?
   _____
   _____

The Man, the Boy, and the Donkey

One day, a farmer and his son were leading their donkey to market. As they came near the town, they passed a villager who laughed at them. "Why are you walking? You have a donkey; you should ride!"

The man put the boy on the donkey, and they continued on their way. They passed another villager who said, "Look at that lazy boy! He rides while his father walks!" So the farmer got on the donkey with his son, and they rode on together.

As they came into the village, a group of villagers laughed at them. "Look at those lazy farmers! They'll break that poor donkey's back!"

The farmer and his son talked about what they could do. They found a long pole, tied the donkey's feet to it, and together they carried the donkey. When they were crossing the Market Bridge, the donkey got one of its feet loose and kicked. This caused the farmers to drop the donkey into the river. Since its feet were tied together, the donkey couldn't swim, and it soon drowned.

"That will teach you," said an old man who had followed them. "Try to please everyone and you will please no one."

After Reading

1. Where were the farmers going?

_____

2. Why did the farmers carry the donkey?

_____

_____

 **Reader's Theater**

In groups of seven, first read through the script silently. Then identify the roles in the story and divide them among you. Each reader should mark his or her lines by underlining or highlighting them.

Read the script together a few times to practice. Ask your teacher about any words you don't know or can't pronounce. Be sure to read your lines at the right time. That means you have to listen carefully to the other readers. Also be sure to read your lines with the appropriate feeling or emotion for your character.

The Man, the Boy, and the Donkey
< Characters: Farmer, Farmer's Son, Villager 1, Villager 2, Villager 3, Villager 4, Narrator >

Scene 1

Narrator: A farmer and his son were leading their donkey to market. The farmer planned to sell the donkey and use the money as a down payment on a truck. As they came close to the village, they met a villager.

Villager 1: Hey, farmer, what's the matter with you? Don't you know that donkeys are for riding? One of you should ride that donkey.

Farmer: Oh, that's right! Son, get up on the donkey and ride.

Son: Yes, Papa!

Narrator: The farmer and his son went on their way, with the boy riding on the donkey. Then they met another villager.

Scene 2

Villager 2: Look at that lazy boy! He makes his father walk while he rides.

Farmer: I guess you're right. Son, get off the donkey and let me ride!

Narrator: So the boy got off and the father got on. They went a little farther and met another villager.

88

Scene 3

Villager 3: Shame on you, farmer! You ride in comfort while your poor son has to walk! You should let him ride, too.

Narrator: The farmer was very embarrassed. He got off the donkey. Then he placed his son in front of him on the donkey and they both rode on.

Villager 4: Look at those lazy bums!

Villager 1: That looks like animal abuse!

Villager 3: Yeah! Two big heavy farmers on one little donkey! They'll break the poor animal's back!

Villager 2: Yeah, the lazy bums!

Villager 4: What's the matter, farmers? Do you want to kill that donkey?

Villager 1: Yeah! What did that poor donkey ever do to you?

Scene 4

Farmer: Son, those villagers are right. We don't want to hurt our donkey.

Son: That's right, Papa. But what can we do?

Farmer: I know what we can do! See that pole over there? We can tie the donkey's front and back legs together, turn him upside down, and carry him with the pole.

Son: Good idea, Dad. Then he'll be fresh and rested when we sell him.

Narrator: So the farmer and his son did just that: they got the pole, tied the donkey's feet to it, and lifted him on their shoulders. They continued on towards the market. All the villagers laughed at them, but the farmer and his son were working too hard to notice. Then they came to the bridge that led to the market.

Scene 5

Son: This donkey is too heavy! It's killing me! Can't we take a break?

Farmer: Hang on, son; we're almost there.

But be careful when we cross the bridge. It's really narrow, and there is no railing.

Son: I can't hold him, Dad! You gave me the heavy end!

Farmer: Watch out! Watch out! He's slipping!

Son: He's trying to kick! Help! Help!

Narrator: The pole slid off the boy's shoulder and the donkey fell off the narrow bridge and into the water with a tremendous splash. The donkey's feet were tied together, so he couldn't swim. He soon sank into the river. The villagers heard the noise and came running.

Farmer: Oh, no! Our donkey is drowning!

Son: He's sinking like a stone!

Farmer: Oh, no! He's gone!

Son: Nothing but bubbles!

Farmer and Son: Now we've lost our donkey! It's YOUR fault, villagers! You made us carry him!

Villager 3: We didn't make you do anything!

Villager 2: Yeah! We have a right to express our opinions!

Villager 4: Yeah! You didn't have to listen to us!

Villager 1: Yeah! That's what you get for trying to please everyone.

All the villagers: Don't you know? If you try to please everyone, you'll end up pleasing no one!

- THE END -

After Performance Questions

1. What happened to the donkey?

2. Why did the farmers carry the donkey?

3. How would you describe the farmer and his son?

4. How would you describe the villagers?

PEOPLE-PLEASER

People-pleasers are people who have low self-esteem or lack confidence. They feel that they always have to please others so that people will like them. Often they have a lot of stress. They are so busy pleasing others that they don't take care of themselves.

People-pleaser Quiz	almost always	often	some-times	almost never
1. I worry about hurting others' feelings.				
2. I have a hard time ending conversations.				
3. I say "yes" when I really want to say "no."				
4. I think I am responsible for others' happiness.				
5. I avoid conflicts and disagreements at all costs.				
6. I feel guilty when I say "no."				
7. I am afraid of being called "selfish."				

Writing & Discussion Projects

1. Pretend that you are the farmer in the fable.
   Take the People-pleaser quiz on page 92. Answer the questions as you think the farmer would answer.

2. "One of the most liberating things we learn in life is that we don't have to like everyone, and everyone doesn't have to like us." Do you agree with this statement? Why or why not?

3. Make a list of all the things you like about yourself.

4. Helping others is a good thing. Is this different from wanting to please everyone? Why or why not?

5. One of the students in your class is wang-dda (왕따). You feel sorry for him or her, but you don't want to be wang-dda yourself. What can you do?

6. What could the donkey say? Write some lines for the donkey to say and put them in the script. Perform the script with the new lines. (Another option would be to retell the story from the Donkey's point of view.)

ABC Grammar & Vocabulary Focus

* Grammar

The modals should, have to/must, and can all have different and distinct meanings.

"Should" refers to advisability and desirability. It means "this is a good idea."

- You should see a dentist often.
- All students should get enough rest.

"Have to/Must" refers to necessity or obligation. You don't have a choice.

- Young men in Korea must do military service.
- Korean students have to study a lot.

"Can" refers to possibility. You are allowed to do something, but you don't have to do it.

- In Korea, you can buy cigarettes when you are 19 years old, but you shouldn't smoke because it's bad for your health.
- In Korea, you can vote when you are 19 years old. You are not permitted to vote when you are younger than 19.

> Teachers can help their students find examples of "can/could" or "can't/couldn't" in the script. Students can also find one example of "have to" and two examples of "should."

> "Should" is used for general advice:
> You should always drive defensively in Seoul.
>
> "Had better" is used for specific advice:
> You had better slow down. I see a traffic jam up ahead.
>
> "Should be" and "must be" can both refer to predictability.
> They can both substitute for "probably is."
> Someone's at the door. That should be the deliveryman.
> Someone's at the door. That must be the deliveryman.
> Someone's at the door. That probably is the deliveryman.

* Vocabulary

A down payment
the money you give at first when you are buying something in installments

A splash
what happens when something is thrown or falls into water

* Expressions/idioms

Lazy bums
an insulting term

To sink like a stone
to disappear quickly after falling or jumping into deep water

To take a break
to stop working for a short period in order to rest

"Hang on!"
words of encouragement, meaning "Don't give up!"
or "Don't stop!" or "Keep waiting! Help will arrive soon!" or "Just a minute!"

CHAPTER

7

THE GRASSHOPPER AND THE ANTS

CHAPTER

7

THE GRASSHOPPER AND THE ANTS

Before Reading

Share your answers to these questions in small groups.

1. If you could have <u>one piece</u> of candy right now or <u>two pieces</u> if you waited for twenty minutes, what would you choose?

   _____
   _____

2. If your friend didn't study at all for a big test and then asked to borrow your notes, what would you do?

   _____
   _____
   _____

The Grasshopper and the Ants

In a field one summer's day a Grasshopper was hopping about, chirping and singing to his heart's content. An Ant passed by, struggling to carry a huge grain of rice back to her nest.

"Why don't you come and sing with me," said the Grasshopper, " instead of working so hard like that?"

"I am helping to store food for the winter," said the Ant, " and I recommend that you do the same."

"Why bother about winter?" said the Grasshopper.
"There's plenty of food right now, and the weather is great."
But the Ant went on her way and continued to work.

When winter came the Grasshopper had no food, and found himself dying of hunger, while the ants had plenty to eat. Then he knew: It is best to prepare for the days of necessity.

After Reading

1. What did the grasshopper do during the summer?

_____

2. Why did the ants have food during the winter?

_____

_____

 **Reader's Theater**

In groups of four, first read through the script silently. Then identify the roles in the story and divide them among you. Each reader should mark his or her lines by underlining or highlighting them.

Read the script together a few times to practice. Ask your teacher about any words you don't know or can't pronounce. Be sure to read your lines at the right time. That means you have to listen carefully to the other readers. Also be sure to read your lines with the appropriate feeling or emotion for your character.

The Grasshopper and the Ants [15]
< Characters: Father Grasshopper, Daughter Grasshopper, Mother Ant, Son Ant >

Scene 1

Daughter Grasshopper: Daddy, I'm hungry! Don't we have any food?

Father Grasshopper: Look in the refrigerator.
   I think we still have some leftover pizza from Pizza School.

Daughter Grasshopper: We ate that yesterday! It was only half a slice!
   I'm starving!

Father Grasshopper: Well, come on. We'll go see the Ants.
   They'll give us some food.

Scene 2

Daughter Grasshopper: I'm so embarrassed! I hate asking the Ants for food.

Father Grasshopper: Just let me do the talking . . . (knocking on the door) . . .
   Knock, knock! Is anybody home?

---

15 This script is based on a script by Kim Jin, Kyoung Jisook, and Park Shinyoung.

Son Ant: Mom, someone is knocking on the door.

Mother Ant: I'll get it. You keep studying. Who is it?

Father Grasshopper: This is Mr. Hopper!

Mother Ant (opening the door): How are you, Mr. Hopper?

Father Grasshopper: Not great, actually.
I came here to ask you for some food. It's winter and I can't find any food at home. My daughter is starving. Could you please help us?

Mother Ant: Oh, no! What did you do with yourself all last summer? Why didn't you collect a store of food for the winter?

Father Grasshopper: Well, I was so busy singing that I didn't have the time. But I wrote some good songs.

Mother Ant: That can't be an excuse for not working.

Daughter Grasshopper (crying): Please, Mrs. Ant! I'm hungry!

Mother Ant: Well, this is the last time I'll give you food.

Father and Daughter Grasshopper: Thank you, Mrs. Ant!

Scene 3

Son Ant: Mom, this homework is so boring! Can't I go outside and play?

Mother Ant: You cannot! Don't you see how the grasshoppers are always begging for food?

Son Ant: But I'm sick and tired of working and studying, studying and working! We never have any fun! I don't want to live like you!

Mother Ant: If you don't work hard, you can't feed yourself and your life will be miserable.

Son Ant: I'm miserable now! Have you noticed that I have no friends?

Mother Ant: OK, then, seeing is believing!
Let's go to the grasshoppers' house. I'll show you how miserable their life is. Come with me!

Scene 4

Mother Ant: Here we are at the grasshopper's house.
Let's just look through the window. They won't see us. Look at them! Do they look happy?

Son Ant: Yes, Mom. They are singing and dancing.
That's the life I want to live!

Daughter Grasshopper: Oh, look who's here! Daddy, we have guests outside!

Father Grasshopper (opening the door): What a nice surprise! Welcome! Come on in!

Mother Ant (hesitating): I'm afraid we can't . . . we have to be going . . .

Son Ant (going inside): Thanks, Mr. Hopper! Come on, Mom! It's warm in here!

Mother Ant (reluctantly): Well, OK. Just for a minute then.

Father Ant: Would you like to dance with us?

Mother Ant: No dancing for me. Listen! I want to say something to you.
My son has always worked hard, but these days he has changed. He doesn't want to study. Instead, he wants to sing and dance, just like your daughter. I think you need to educate your daughter properly.

Father Grasshopper: What do you mean by "educate properly"?
All parents have their own philosophy. Have you never heard that all work and no play makes Jack a dull boy? I think your son is very wise. He doesn't want to be a dull boy. Think about it.
Are you happy with your life?

Mother Ant: I think our life is better than yours.
   At least we don't beg for food.

Daughter Grasshopper: Dad, come and play a song for us!

Son Ant: Mom, come and dance with us! Let's have some fun. Please . . .

Father Ant: Yes, Mrs. Ant. You deserve a break.
   How about having some fun with us? I'll sing my new song for you.
   You've been so kind to us. Let me return the favor!

Mother Ant (reluctantly): Well . . . OK.

Son Ant (dancing): Mom, don't you love his aesthetic?

Mother Ant: What?

Son Ant: Uh . . . this is cool, isn't it?

Mother Ant (dancing): Yes it really is! It's almost as cool as "Shabang, Shabang!" Hey, I've got an idea! Mr. Hopper, how about singing songs down at the Anthill Factory while the ants are working? Then we can share food and songs.

Father Grasshopper: Great idea! I like that!

Daughter Grasshopper: Awesome! I don't have to be hungry anymore.

Son Ant: And my life will be happier.
   I can take a break when I get too burned out!

Father Grasshopper: I think I found a new philosophy!

Mother Ant: What's that, Mr. Hopper?

Father Grasshopper: Don't work or play your life away – a happy life needs work AND play!

- THE END -

After Performance Questions

1. What was Mrs. Ant's idea?

2. Why did Mrs. Ant want Mr. Hopper to educate his daughter properly?

3. Do you think that Daughter Grasshopper was a good influence or a bad influence on Son Ant?

Writing & Discussion Projects

1. Do you think it is right to do no work and expect others to pick up the tab? Why or why not?

2. Do you agree that "all work and no play makes Jack a dull boy (or Jill a dull girl)"? Why or why not?

3. What are some ways to take a break from studying?

4. On the next page, read Wilma Jalkanen's daily schedule (adapted from http://www.timeforkids.com/destination/finland/day-in-life). **Wilma is a student in Helsinki, Finland. Write her an email introducing yourself and telling her about your daily schedule.**
You can also ask her questions about her schedule.

Wilma Jalkanen
11 years old – 6th grader – lives in Helsinki, Finland

7:30 am	I wake up, brush my teeth, and get dressed.
7:45 am	I eat breakfast with my brothers, Vaino and August. Sometimes Mom makes me a fried egg. Sometimes I eat toast or yogurt.
8:20 am	I ride my bike to the metro station. It takes about 5 minutes. I ride the metro to school (15 minutes). Sometimes the train is packed, so I can't find a seat.
8:45 am	I meet my friends at the metro stop close to school. We walk to school together, talking about books or movies.
9:00 am	My first class is math class. We are learning to add and subtract fractions.
9:50 am	Today, we go outside for science class. We examine different tree types.
10:50 am	I eat lunch at the school cafeteria (lunch is free for all students in Finland). Today we have macaroni with sausage sauce. My favorite lunch is tortillas.
12:00 pm	I have French class. After that, I have homework class, where we do homework with a teacher's help. My teacher is funny and not too strict.
1:30 pm	In computer class, I create a slide show about medieval times for history class.
2:15 pm	School is over. My friend and I ride the metro back home. From my stop, I ride my bike back to my house.
3:00 pm	My dog Panda welcomes me back. I play with Panda and have a snack.
3:30 pm	I do homework in my room for 15 minutes. Then I practice my flute before leaving for drama club. We rehearse for our performance.
8:30 pm	I come back home after a long day. My dad has made fajitas. I eat supper, wash up, brush my teeth, and go to bed.

5. Using the chart below, write a dialogue between a Korean student and a Finnish student in which the two students talk about their schools and ask each other questions. You should give names to the students in your dialogue. Some Finnish boy's names are Mikko, Juho, and Aleksi. Some Finnish girl's names are Anna, Veera, and Emilia. The chart was adapted from "South Korea's School Success" by Deva Dalporto on the We Are Teachers website at

http://www.weareteachers.com/blogs/post/2015/04/01/south-korea-s-school-success

	South Korea	Finland
Study Time	School Hours 9am - 5pm Night classes Hagwon classes	School Hours 9am - 2pm Very little homework
Testing	many tests KSAT	only one standardized test
Academic pressure	Students are under extreme pressure to get good grades. Their future depends on getting a good score on the KSAT.	Students and teachers don't care much about marks. Finnish schools emphasize learning by doing and building community.
Use of technology	South Korea leads the world in educational technology	Finnish schools don't have a lot of technology. Students in Finland often study outdoors.
Recess	Students don't have recess.	In Finland they believe in giving the kids a lot of playtime. Students get 75 minutes of recess per day.
Educational Philosophy	Education is the pathway to success.	Education is a life-long adventure.
Success in international exams	top scores	top scores

 **Grammar & Vocabulary Focus**

* Grammar (Advanced)

1. Verbs with infinitives and/or gerunds

Some verbs can be followed by an infinitive (to + base form).

- I want to watch TV.
- I need to do my homework.
- I hope to visit Australia when I'm older.
- My friends and I agreed to study together.

Some verbs can be followed by a gerund (base form + ing).

- I enjoy dancing.
- I dislike doing homework.
- I considered moving to America, but then Donald Trump was elected.
- The politician denied lying about his income taxes.

Some verbs can be followed by either an infinitive or a gerund.

- I like listening to music. I like to listen to music.
- I love ice skating. I love to ice skate.
- I hate asking the ants for food. I hate to ask the ants for food.
- I prefer watching TV. I prefer to watch TV.

> This aspect of English is very tricky. Students need to get a lot of experience through extensive reading and noticing the features of different verbs. Teachers can help their students to find examples of verbs with infinitives or gerunds in the script and in other readings.

2. See, Watch, Look at

"See" and "Watch" have different meanings and uses.
(In Korean, both meanings are expressed by 보다.)

"See" means that something becomes visible to someone.
There is NO definite intention or choice on the part of the person who sees.

- My wife is sad when she sees old people pushing recycling carts on the street.
- In Itaewon, you can see people from many different countries.
- I saw how tired my students were, so I let them go home a little early.
- We can see the mountain from our hotel room.

"Watch" implies intention and choice on the part of the watcher.

- I used to watch CSI on TV, but I stopped watching it because I had seen all the episodes more than five times.
- The researcher watched the chimpanzees for hours, but they didn't do anything unusual.
- "A watched pot never boils." (Proverbial expression)

"Look at" also implies intention and choice, but for a shorter duration.

- That man is looking at the mountain.
- That driver is looking at his phone, not the street.
- "A cat may look at a king." (Proverbial expression)

> Teachers can help their students to find an example of the contrast between "see" and "watch" in the script.

* Vocabulary

A philosophy
In this case, the personal values and beliefs that guide a person's behavior.

Burned out
exhausted from too much work, stress, and/or study

* Expressions/idioms

To return the favor
to do something nice for someone who has done something nice for you

Seeing is believing
Evidence is more convincing than words.

To be a good/bad influence on someone
to have a good/bad effect on someone's behavior or beliefs

"Don't you love his aesthetic?" (slang)
"Don't you love the way his music sounds?"
"Don't you love his music's unique characteristics?"

CHAPTER

ANDROCLES AND THE LION

CHAPTER

ANDROCLES AND THE LION

 ## Before Reading
Share your answers to these questions in small groups.

	Coliseum (Rome)	World Cup Stadium (Seoul)
		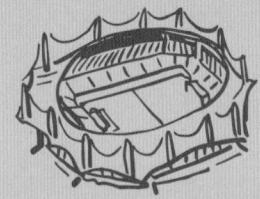
Year Built	completed 80 AD	completed 2001
Number of Seats	80,000	66,704
Events	re-enactments of battles chariot races gladiatorial combats [16] wild beast hunts; executions	soccer (football) matches concerts festivals Korean traditional performances

1. Look at the chart above. It compares the Coliseum in ancient Rome with the World Cup Stadium in Seoul. If you had the power to travel in time, would you rather attend an event at the Roman Coliseum or at Seoul World Cup Stadium? What event would you attend? Why?

   _____
   _____

2. a. Do you know anyone who has moved to Korea to live?

   _____
   _____

   b. Do you know anyone who has moved to another country to live?

   _____
   _____

   c. What are some reasons why people move to another country to live?

   _____
   _____
   _____

---

16 Gladiatorial combats – fights between gladiators.
    A gladiator was a slave who was forced to fight with a sword (gladius) or other weapon for the amusement of spectators.

Androcles and the Lion

Androcles was a slave in ancient Rome. He was not a free man; he belonged to his master. Whenever his master wanted something, he said,
"Androcles, do this!" or "Androcles, bring me that!" and Androcles had to obey . . . or else!

One day, Androcles had had enough. Early the next morning, before anyone else was awake, he crept quietly out of the room where the slaves slept. He went quickly through the town and into the woods. Then he started running for his life, because he knew what the Romans did to runaway slaves. He ran through the forests and he ran through the marshes and he ran through the stony mountains until he was so tired he couldn't run anymore. Then he saw a cave in the side of a mountain.
"I can rest in there," thought Androcles.

Androcles went into the cave, collapsed in a corner, and soon was fast asleep. He woke up to the sound of heavy breathing and growling. Something else was in the cave! He opened his eyes, and his blood froze. Not two meters away was an enormous lion, lying between him and the mouth of the cave.

Androcles looked around for something he could use as a weapon, but the lion made no move to attack him. Androcles saw that the lion was growling in pain as it tore at its front paw with its teeth. Stuck in the paw was a huge thorn. Androcles cautiously went closer to the lion. Its paw was red and swollen. "Well," thought Androcles, "this poor lion has his troubles, too. " Summoning all his courage, he grabbed the thorn and pulled it out of the lion's paw. As the lion growled and licked his paw, Androcles ran past the lion and out of the cave.

Meanwhile, Roman soldiers had been following Androcles and were waiting for him outside the cave. They captured him, put him in chains, and took him back to Rome, where he was sentenced to die in the Coliseum. When the day for his execution came, the soldiers led him into the Coliseum. A large crowd of spectators [17] was there, including the Emperor and his entourage.[18] As the crowd cheered, a huge lion came rushing and roaring towards him. When the lion reached Androcles, however, it stopped roaring and licked his hand. It was the same lion that Androcles had helped in the cave. The Emperor was very surprised and demanded to know why the lion was so friendly to Androcles, so Androcles told him the whole story. The Emperor was so impressed by Androcles' story that he gave him his freedom.

After Reading

1. Where did Androcles live?

_____

2. Why did the lion not eat Androcles?

_____

_____

3. Why did the Emperor give Androcles his freedom?

_____

_____

17 Spectators – people who have come to be entertained by watching some event
18 Entourage (on-too-'razh) – the advisors and companions that accompany a powerful person.

 **Reader's Theater**

In groups of seven, first read through the script silently. Then identify the roles in the story and divide them among you. Each reader should mark his or her lines by underlining or highlighting them.

Read the script together a few times to practice. Ask your teacher about any words you don't know or can't pronounce. Be sure to read your lines at the right time. That means you have to listen carefully to the other readers. Also be sure to read your lines with the appropriate feeling or emotion for your character.

Androcles and the Lion

<Characters: Narrator 1, Narrator 2, Androcles, Roman Soldier 1, Roman Soldier 2, Judge, Emperor >

Scene 1

Narrator 1: Androcles was a slave in ancient Rome. He was not a free person like you or I. He belonged to his master. Whenever his master wanted something, he said, "Androcles, do this!" or "Androcles, bring me that!" and Androcles had to obey immediately . . . or his master would beat him.

Narrator 2: One day, Androcles had had enough. His master had beaten him for spilling some wine as he poured it into his master's glass. That night, as Androcles lay in the room where the house slaves slept, feeling the pain of the wounds on his back, he decided to run away.

Narrator 1: Early the next morning, before anyone else was awake, he crept quietly out of the room where the slaves slept. He went quickly through the town and into the woods. Then he started running for his life, because he knew what the Romans did to runaway slaves. He ran through the forests and he ran through the marshes and he ran through the stony mountains until he was so tired that he couldn't run anymore. Then he saw a cave in the side of a mountain.

Androcles: I've got to rest. I can't run any more. I'll hide in that cave.

Narrator 2: Androcles went into the cave, collapsed in a corner, and soon was fast asleep. Meanwhile, the Roman soldiers that had been tracking Androcles through the forests and the marshes came into the mountains.

Scene 2

Roman Soldier 1: Look over here, sir! I've found his trail! See the tracks in the dirt.

Roman Soldier 2: They lead up to that cave in the mountain. Come on!

Roman Soldier 1: That accurséd slave made me miss my breakfast! We've been chasing him all day. Now we have to climb all the way up to that cave.

Roman Soldier 2: Don't worry! When we catch him, he'll pay for that!

Roman Soldier 1: Coliseum time!

Scene 3

Narrator 2: Androcles, sleeping in the cave, woke up to the sound of heavy breathing and growling. Something else was in the cave!

Androcles: What's that? It sounds like a big animal!

Narrator 1: Androcles opened his eyes, and his blood froze. Not two meters away from him was an enormous lion, lying between him and the mouth of the cave.

Androcles: Oh, no! Did I escape from slavery just to be eaten by a lion? Is there a big stick or a rock here, anything I can use as a weapon?

Narrator 2: Androcles looked around for something he could use as a weapon, but the lion made no move to attack him.

Androcles: Why doesn't the lion attack? It seems to be in pain. It's licking and chewing at its front paw. Oh, I see what's going on! A huge thorn is stuck in its paw. Poor lion! You have your troubles, too. Don't bite me; I'm here to help you.

Narrator 1: Summoning all his courage, Androcles grabbed the thorn and pulled it out of the lion's paw. As the lion growled and licked its paw, Androcles ran past the lion and out of the cave. But the soldiers were waiting for him.

Scene 4

Roman Soldier 1: Freeze, slave! Make a move and I'll spear you!

Narrator 2: Androcles, preferring to die than to be captured, tried to run, but one of the soldiers hit him with the butt end of his spear and knocked him out.

Roman Soldier 2: We've got you now, slave! Put those chains on him. Let's take him back to Rome.

Roman Soldier 1: Coliseum time!

Scene 5

Narrator 1: Back in Rome, Androcles was brought before a judge who sentenced him to die in the Coliseum.

Judge: In the name of the senate and the people of Rome, I sentence you to be torn apart by wild beasts as a lesson to any slave who dares to escape! Long live the Emperor!

Narrator 2: The soldiers took Androcles to the Coliseum and threw him into a tiny cell to wait for his execution.

Narrator 1: Soon the fateful day came.
A grand combat[19] of gladiators was scheduled in the Coliseum to celebrate the Emperor's recent victories in Gaul.[20] Before the gladiators fought, some run-away slaves and other criminals would be put to death as a warm-up. All of Rome, including the Emperor and his court, poured into[21] the Coliseum to watch the grand spectacle.[22]

Narrator 2: Androcles was scheduled to die first, which was lucky for him because he wouldn't have to listen to the screams of the others while he waited. When the Emperor and his court were all settled in their box seats and all the announcements had been made, the soldiers went to Androcles' cell.

Scene 6

Roman Soldier 1: Wake up, slave! It's Coliseum time!

Roman Soldier 2: Come on, slave; get up! I hear they caught a new lion. It's very fierce! They've been starving it so it will be really happy to see you!

Roman Soldier 1: Really, really happy!

Roman Soldier 2: Come on, lion food! Your time's up!

Narrator 1: The soldiers dragged Androcles into the Coliseum and left him. He heard someone shout, "Release the lion!" and then the crowd started yelling and cheering. The noise was deafening, but Androcles barely heard it. He felt like he was in a dream. He resolved to die bravely.

Narrator 2: An enormous lion, roaring fiercely, came rushing toward Androcles. Suddenly it stopped, looked at Androcles, and started to lick his hand.

Androcles (surprised and relieved): It's you, old friend! So they caught you, too, huh?

Narrator 1: It was the lion that Androcles had helped. The crowd and the Emperor were astounded. Who was this slave that could tame wild beasts? The Emperor commanded the soldiers to bring Androcles before his Imperial Box. The lion went along with Androcles, looking hungrily at the nervous soldiers.

19 A combat of gladiators – a battle between two groups of gladiators
20 Gaul – a Roman province, now called France
21 Poured into the Coliseum – came into the Coliseum at about the same time
22 Spectacle – an extravagant show

Emperor: Slave! You have cheated your Fate, at least for now! How is it that this wild beast fawns[23] upon you, licking your hand and gazing[24] at you like a puppy gazes at its master?

Androcles: Well, it's like this, Your Majesty!

Narrator 2: Androcles told the Emperor the whole story. When he was finished, the Emperor was silent for a moment and then spoke in his solemn Emperor voice as the whole Coliseum listened.

Emperor (slowly and solemnly): If a man can show mercy to a lion, and a lion can show mercy to a man, then your Emperor, who is a Lion among men, can show mercy also! Slave, you are free! Take this purse of gold and return to your home country. Soldiers! Take this lion into the forest and set it free!

Roman Soldier 1: But, Your Majesty! I don't think this lion likes us very much.

Emperor: Do as your Emperor commands! And by the way, all the other slaves can go free also!

Roman Soldier 2 (very surprised): Really, Your Majesty?

Emperor: No, I was only kidding! I don't want to ruin our economy. But let Androcles go free.

Roman Soldier 1 & 2: It shall be as you command! Long live the Emperor!

Androcles: And long live Androcles and the Lion!

- THE END -

---

23 Fawns upon you – treats you with respect and affection; flatters you
24 Gazing at you – looking at you

❓ After Performance Questions

1. Why didn't the Romans feed the lion?

   _____

   _____

2. Why did Androcles run away from his master?

   _____

   _____

3. Why were the Roman soldiers afraid of the lion?

   _____

   _____

 # Writing & Discussion Projects

1. Retell the story from the Lion's point of view.

2. Do online research with your group about modern slavery. Then give a short group presentation on what you have learned. These websites have good information that you can use:

   • https://www.amnesty.org.uk/sites/default/files/activities_-_slavery_today_english_0.pdf

   • http://www.antislavery.org/english/what_we_do/education/resources_for_education/case_studies_images.aspx

3. Read the three biographies [25] of modern slaves on pages 123 and 124. Choose one biography and write a short Reader's Theater script about that person's life.

4. Write a letter of encouragement from Androcles to a modern slave.

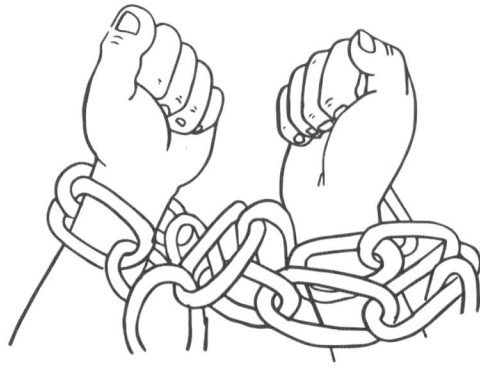

---

25 Biography (by- 'og- ruh- fee) – the story of a person's life

Modern Slave Biographies

Read these three biographies and choose one.
Write a Reader's Theater script that tells that person's story.

* Vocabulary

Human trafficking
an organized criminal activity in which human beings are treated as possessions to be controlled and exploited

Trafficker
a member of a human trafficking gang

To smuggle
to bring people or goods into a country illegally

Captors
people who have captured someone and are keeping him or her as a prisoner

A domestic slave
a person who is forced to cook and clean without being paid for his or her labor

---

1. Miriam – Ivory Coast; the United States
Miriam's story is adapted from a case study on the website "Learning about Modern Slavery" at http://bjmolzahn-curric371.weebly.com/case-studies.html

---

Miriam grew up with her family in Ivory Coast, Africa. Her family was very poor.
She dreamed of getting an education and having a better life.

Some men offered to take her to the United States, where she could go to school in return for doing some domestic labor. She went to the United States, but found out that the men had tricked her. She was forced to be a domestic slave.

For five years she worked every day for up to 20 hours. She never got paid. Her captors told her they were sending money back to her parents, but they were lying. She never had a day off and wasn't allowed to contact her family in Ivory Coast.

Two months after her best friend escaped, Miriam decided to escape as well. With the help of another friend, she escaped and told the police about the traffickers. They were arrested, tried, and sentenced to five years in prison.

Miriam is now free, working and sending money to her family. She dreams of becoming a nurse so that she can help people.

2. Li Wei – China; the United Kingdom

Li Wei's story is adapted from a case study on the Amnesty International "Slavery Today" website at https://www.amnesty.org.uk/sites/default/files/activities_-_slavery_today_english_0.pdf

In China, poor families sometimes sell their male children to "snakehead" gangs who promise to take the boys to a better life in a new country. The gangs charge a high price for their services, sometimes as much as $40,000 (40 million won).

Once the child is smuggled to a new country, he has to work to pay off the debt that his family owes. This is called "debt bondage."

Li Wei was sold to a "snakehead" gang when he was 10 years old. They brought him to England and made him work in a restaurant seven days a week. He slept in a shed with other boys from China.

When he was 16, he ran away from the restaurant. He had nowhere to go and didn't speak English. The English police found him sleeping outside and took him to the local Social Services. Social Services placed him in a foster home.

A few days later, some men came to the foster home and claimed to be Li Wei's uncles. The foster parent did not tell them that Li Wei lived there and told Social Services about their visit. Social Services moved him to a new foster home; he agreed not to tell his "uncles" where he was.

3. Grace – Tanzania; the United Kingdom

Grace's story is adapted from a case study on the Amnesty International "Slavery Today" website at https://www.amnesty.org.uk/sites/default/files/activities_-_slavery_today_english_0.pdf

After Grace's parents died, she worked at a market stall in Dodoma, Tanzania. One day the woman who ran the stall told her to go with two men. She told Grace that the men would take her to live abroad, where she could go to school.

The men took her to the United Kingdom, where she was taken to a house and locked in the kitchen. Grace was forced to live in this room for two years. By climbing on a chair, she could just see into a garden. She had no idea where she was. Grace was forced to clean and cook for her "owner," who was later joined by another man. They treated her very badly.

One day, one of the men got drunk and failed to lock the kitchen door. She ran away. The man woke up and chased her, but she hid in a ditch and managed to flag down [26] a car. The driver took her to a police station in London.

(Student writers can complete Grace's story.)

---

[26] To flag down a car – to successfully signal the driver of the car to stop and help you

 Grammar & Vocabulary Focus

* Grammar (Advanced)

1. Past Perfect (had + past participle)

Use the past perfect to describe an action that was completed before another past action.

- As Androcles lay in his bed, he thought about how his master had beaten him for spilling some wine.
- I had just finished my homework when my friend called and invited me to meet him.

2. Past Perfect Progressive (had + been + present participle)

Use the past perfect progressive to describe a continuing action that was completed before another past action.

- The Romans had been starving the lion, so it was very hungry when it came into the Coliseum.
- I had been working on my homework for about an hour when my friend called.

> Teachers can help their students find examples of Past Perfect and Past Perfect Continuous in the script. There are three examples of Past Perfect and one example of Past Perfect Continuous. There is also one example of Present Perfect Continuous.

* Vocabulary

To fawn upon someone

to exhibit a lot of affection towards someone, as a dog might show to its owner. Also: to flatter someone.

To be astounded

to be very surprised

To gaze at someone or something

to look at someone or something very intently

The butt end of his spear

the non-pointy end of his spear

* Expressions/idioms

Androcles summoned all his courage

Androcles tried very hard to be brave. To summon someone is to order that person to come to you. Figuratively, Androcles ordered his courage to come to him.

"How is it that this wild beast fawns upon you?"

Why does this wild beast fawn upon you?

"The crowd poured into the Coliseum"

the crowd came into the Coliseum together." This is another figurative expression. Literally, the verb "to pour" means "to transfer liquid from one container to another," as in "My uncle poured soju into my grandfather's glass." In the literal usage, "to pour" requires an object. In the figurative usage, "the crowd" requires a prepositional phrase: "The fans poured out of the stadium when the game was over."

To flag down a car

to successfully signal a car to stop (The person who flags down the car is probably standing beside the road and waving his or her arms to signal the driver to stop.)

CHAPTER

WRITING OUR OWN SCRIPTS

CHAPTER

WRITING OUR OWN SCRIPTS

Purpose of this Chapter

For our students to experience the motivational and language-learning benefits of Reader's Theater, the scripts should be lively, interesting, and dramatically effective. This chapter is for teachers who want to write or adapt their own scripts, or who want to give guidance to students who are doing one of the script-writing projects in this book.

Teachers are encouraged to write or adapt their own scripts for the following reasons. (1) Teachers can personalize the scripts by including details that are relevant to their students, such as details about their school or contemporary culture. (2) They can choose stories, such as Korean folk tales, for which Reader's Theater versions might not exist. (3) Since fables and folktales are usually set in ancient times, teachers can modernize the setting or the situation to make the story more engaging, relevant, or comprehensible. (4) Teachers can write or adapt scripts to fit a particular lesson, either in terms of form or content.

Teachers can also use this chapter to guide their students in writing their own scripts. The purposes of the script writing projects in this book are (1) to give students opportunities for meaningful language production and (2) to give them opportunities to develop creativity and critical thinking. For the second purpose especially, teachers need to consider how to give feedback to students.

In *Creativity in the Classroom*, Alane Jordan Starko (2010) distinguishes between two types of feedback. One type, controlling feedback (such as "Good work!" or "You can do better!"), lets students know "where they stand in the teacher's eyes and probably how they stand in relation to others in the class." This type of evaluative feedback, whether positive or negative, tends to inhibit creativity (249).

The other type of feedback is informational feedback. It "assumes that students are in charge of organizing and evaluating their own learning. It provides useful information for their guidance" (249). The next pages give some tips for writing scripts that will be fun to perform and watch, supported by examples from the scripts in this book (teachers are of course welcome to add their own ideas to this list).

Teachers should take care to impart these tips lightly, however: if students are working happily and creatively, they perhaps should not be interrupted, despite the teacher's judgement that what they are doing is not dramatically sound. After all, our goal is to encourage them to produce language, personalize, and develop their creativity.

Rather than just giving students informational feedback in a teacher-centered way, it might be helpful to scaffold them and help them explore creative possibilities through brainstorming and discussion activities. That is the goal of the "Fox and the Grapes" activity on page 135.

Tips for turning an Aesop's Fable or other folk story into an effective Reader's Theater script.

1. We can turn narration into dialogue or monologue.

Example: The original version of "Belling the Cat" says that the mice "discussed and rejected plan after plan." The script version shows this happening in dialogue. Because of this, more readers can participate. "Showing" is also more engaging than "telling."

2. We can develop the characters.

Example: The first scene in "The Turtle and the Rabbit" script introduces us to the boastful, over-confident character of the rabbit. The first scene in "The Wind and the Sun" script introduces us to the arrogant, violent character of the Wind. In "The Grasshopper and the Ants," Mrs. Ant is very negative towards the Grasshoppers at first, but then becomes more open to compromise.

3. We can add characters.

Example: In "The Rabbit and the Turtle," the addition of the characters Squirrel, Magpie, and Hedgehog allows more readers to participate and provides more opportunities for interactions and dialogue. These characters are also useful in clarifying plot and action.

4. We can add details and scenes that create dramatic tension.

Example: Dramatic tension is the quality in a drama that enables readers and listeners to identify with the characters, become involved in their story, and care what happens to them. The "Belling the Cat" script begins with a scene that shows that dangers of the cat so that readers perceive the mice's problem as more than an abstract one. The "Lion and the Mouse" script emphasizes what will happen to the Lion if he is captured, and also shows the Buffalo and the Cheetah refusing to help the Lion to increase the tension (action movies extend scenes of danger in the same way; the hero saves the heroine at the last possible moment).

5. We can add humor.

Example: The silly suggestions and excuses of the mice are intended to add humor and make the script more fun for readers and listeners. In "The Rabbit and the Turtle," the Rabbit's teasing, Mrs. Hedgehog's pride in her babies, and the Rabbit's absorption in the computer game are all intended to be humorous.

6. We can add contemporary references or modernize the setting.

Example: The PC Room in "The Rabbit and the Turtle" adds a contemporary reference that students can relate to and be amused by. Contemporary references tend to help students feel validated, to feel that their world and interests are worthy of inclusion in the classroom. "The Grasshopper and the Ants" changes the setting into a modern one wherein the Son Ant is burdened with schoolwork just like the students who will be reading the script. This makes the story and its lesson more real and meaningful for them.

Chapters 3, 4, and 5 each have a Writing or Discussion Project that asks the students to retell the story in a modern setting. These projects are intended to be fun and engaging for the students, to generate production, and to allow personalization. Of course these projects can also help them to develop creativity and critical thinking skills and to relate the script's lesson to their own lives. In a new version of "The Wind and the Sun," the Wind could be a bully in school; in "The Rabbit and the Turtle," the Rabbit could be a student who had lived in an English-speaking country; in "The Lion and the Mouse," the Lion could be a CEO and the Mouse a lowly office-worker. These are just some possibilities that the teacher could suggest if the students needed help (See Appendix 2 for some more ideas). Ideally, the students should have the freedom to develop their own ideas.

7. We can change the plot or the moral.

Example: This possibility is related to #6 above.

The authors of "The Grasshopper and the Ants" changed the lesson into one that they felt more comfortable with. In my writing course, many of my students have changed this particular fable so that some kind of balance between work and play was achieved. Student writers should be encouraged to use script writing to express a lesson that they personally endorse.

Exploring Dramatic Possibilities

Read the fable below.

The Fox and the Grapes

A hungry fox saw some fine bunches of grapes hanging from a vine that was trained along a high trellis, and did his best to reach them by jumping as high as he could in the air. But it was all in vain, for they were just out of reach, so he gave up trying and walked away with an air of dignity and unconcern, remarking, "I thought those grapes were ripe, but I see now that they are quite sour."

 **Now let's read a Readers' Theater script adapted from it.**

The Fox and the Grapes

NARRATOR: A hungry fox saw some fine bunches of grapes hanging from a vine that was trained along a high trellis, and did his best to reach them by jumping as high as he could in the air. But it was all in vain, for they were just out of reach, so he gave up trying and walked away with an air of dignity and unconcern.

FOX: I thought those grapes were ripe, but I see now that they are quite sour.

> Is this script dramatically effective? What can we do to improve it?
> In groups, brainstorm some ways to make the script more fun and lively.

 **Brainstorm in groups and then share ideas in whole class:**

We can add characters: a crow who teases the fox because he can't get the grapes.

We can turn the grapes themselves into a character; they can tease the fox: "You can't get us!" "We're so sweet!"

We can change the story so the fox finds a way to get the grapes. (Then the fox eats them and they really are sour).

We can combine this story with "The fox and the crow" (where a fox tricks a crow into singing so the food she has in her beak falls to the ground).

 **Model script:** Here is a rather conservative adaptation of "The Fox and the Grapes." It doesn't have any big changes, but it does try to build dramatic tension by describing the deliciousness of the grapes. It also adds a character (Dog) so the fox will have someone to interact with and so the fox's character can be developed.

The Fox and the Grapes
<Characters: Fox, Dog>

Scene 1

Fox: Boy, it's hot today! That August sun is like a hammer beating on my head! I could really use a cool drink. Is there a stream around here? Wait . . . what's that in the branches of that tree? Is it a grapevine? Yes, it is! Mmm! Those grapes look delicious – so cool and plump and sweet and juicy! I can even see the drops of dew on their shiny purple skins. Just the thing for a day like this. If I jump high enough, I can grab a mouthful! [The fox jumps]

Scene 2

Dog: Hey Fox, what are you doing?

Fox: I'm getting those grapes up there in that tree. You can't have any! I saw them first.

Dog: You can't get them. They're too high!

Fox: No, they're not. Foxes can jump very high. [The fox jumps again]

Dog: You missed!

[The fox jumps again]

Dog: You missed!

Fox: No, I didn't! What do you mean, "Missed"? I'm just doing my exercises. I don't want those grapes. I never wanted them. Anyone can see that they're sour. See how tiny and hard and green they are. I'll bet they have ants all over them, too! Stupid grapes! If you want them, you can have them. This fox has better things to do with his (her) time!

-THE END –

 **Other possibilities for original scripts:**

1. Write a script or a story about an exciting experience that you once had.

- Your most memorable day
- Your happiest birthday
- Your most enjoyable vacation

2. Write a script or a story that illustrates one of these Korean proverbs:

- 개구리 올챙이 적 생각도 못 한다.
  (The frog doesn't remember when it was a tadpole.)
- 원숭이도 나무에서 떨어질 때가 있다.
  (Even a monkey can fall down from a tree.)
- 빈 수레가 요란하다.
  (When the wagon is empty, it makes more noise.)
- 고양이에게 생선을 맡기다.
  (To let the cat take care of the fish . . .)
  (English proverb: "To let the fox guard the henhouse . . .")
- 예방은 치료약보다 낫다.
  (English proverb: "An ounce of prevention is worth a pound of cure.")

3. Turn a Korean folktale into a script

- The Disobedient Frog
- The Rabbit's Judgement
- Why the Sea is Salty

APPENDIX 1
-
PERFORMANCE NOTES

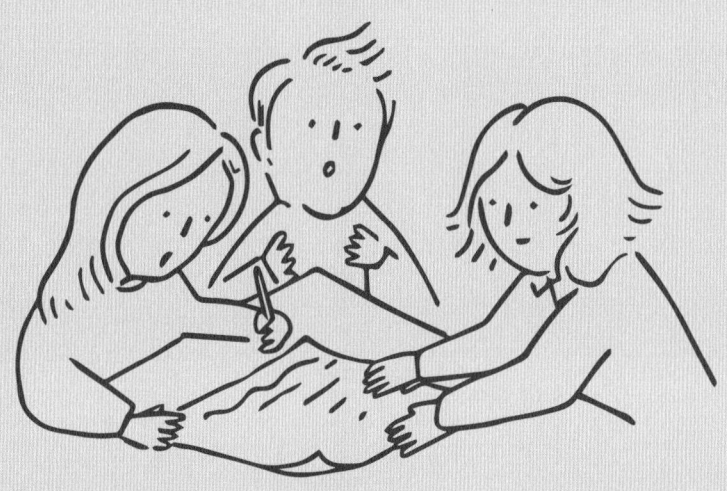

Readers should always keep in mind that they are not reading for each other or for the teacher, but for their classmates.

Reading Suggestions

Readers need a fun and effective script, but they also need to read the script in an engaging way. They should be encouraged to speak clearly and confidently, to look at the audience as much as possible, and to hold their scripts down so that their faces are not hidden [27]. In so doing, they are not only connecting with the audience but also developing confidence and presentation skills.

Reader's Theater does not use elaborate stage movement or blocking, but use of movements that can be done "in place" could be effective, especially if the readers create them on their own. For instance, the student reading the Sun in "The Wind and the Sun" could make a hand gesture to represent sunshine as he/she reads the line "Bling, bling, bling!" Similarly, the readers could dance in place at the appropriate moments in "The Grasshopper and the Ants," or the Mice could pretend to hold a rope and chew it in "The Lion and the Mouse." These movements could increase the readers' and audience's involvement and comprehension while introducing a welcome kinesthetic element.

Finally, a technique that really grabs the audience's attention is for one or more readers to pick a short line from their part and memorize it: they can then look directly at the audience or at the character the line is addressed to as they deliver the line. This adds an element of "realism" that audiences will catch and appreciate.

---

[27] Some Reader's Theater performances follow the convention that readers turn their backs to the audience when they are not speaking and the turn around when they speak their lines; I think that this is overly formal and distracts from the interaction among the characters.

Classroom atmosphere

Readers also need to be engaged with the script and to feel that their self-expression is being appreciated. To help them achieve this, the classroom atmosphere should be both fun and focused. I have observed student presentations in elementary classrooms wherein the rest of the students were unfocused and noisy while other students presented. This took away motivation from the presenters; they presented in a mumbling and perfunctory way, as if they were thinking, "No one is listening; we're just doing this to please the teacher. Let's get it over with as fast as we can and sit down." Moreover, the rest of the class did not get the benefit of any language exposure. To avoid this kind of atmosphere, teachers should carefully manage the class so that the students' attention is directed to the readers, so that the script performances are introduced positively and enthusiastically, and so that students know that they are expected to keep quiet and pay attention to their classmates and that their classmates will pay attention to them when it's their turn to present.

Pronunciation skills

Finally, a Reader's Theater performance is an opportunity for students to work on pronunciation skills, including word and sentence stress. (Of course the teacher should always emphasize that mistakes are OK; everyone makes mistakes, and they present good opportunities to learn more.) Focus on sentence stress can also help with meaning focus, since the meaning focus in an English sentence is indicated by the sentence stress. Here is an example of the same sentence with different sentence stresses and different contextual meanings.

The stress is indicated by the **bold type**.

(1) **I** didn't take your book. (She took it.)
(2) I **didn't** take your book. (I know you think I took it, but I didn't.)
(3) I didn't **take** your book. (I only borrowed it.)
(4) I didn't take **your** book. (I took his book.)
(5) I didn't take your **book**. (I took your smartphone.)

Here are some examples from the scripts:

(1) Mouse 5: We can **shoot** the cat!
    Mouse 4: We don't have a **gun**.

(2) Wind: See? That tree is **bow**ing to me. I'm the **strong**est in the sky!
    Sun: Don't be so **sure**. I think I'm **strong**er than **you**.

Korean sentences also have rhythmical and stress patterns, but they don't work in the same way as English sentences, so this aspect of English phonology needs attention and practice.

A note on using this book with mixed-ability classes

1. Performing the scripts

a. The earlier scripts are shorter and easier than the later ones.
With lower ability classes, it might be better to focus on Chapters 1-4 until you feel your students are ready for longer scripts. In mixed ability classes, students could be grouped according to ability and the different groups could perform appropriately-leveled scripts.

b. Teachers can also assign the roles themselves, giving shorter roles to lower-level students.

2. Discussion Questions and Projects

a. Teachers can choose Writing or Discussion projects that are appropriate to their students' levels; for instance, the Best Advice Game (Ch. 1) would clearly be less challenging than a Presentation about Modern Slavery (Ch. 8). The Retelling Questions (such as "retell the story so the Wind wins") would be manageable for lower-level students as group/whole class discussions.

b. For the discussion, post-reading, and post-performance questions, the teacher could have students work in mixed-level pairs according to collaborative structures such as "Timed Pair Share," wherein the partners share their ideas for a pre-determined amount of time (say one minute). Such collaborative structures ensure that all students participate and allow lower-level students to respond according to their language ability and understanding of the topic while also challenging higher-level students to respond with more in-depth observations (Kagan and Kagan, 2009).

3. Grammar Focus

a. Many of the Grammar Focus sections are aimed at more advanced learners: Past Perfect (Ch.8), Infinitives and Gerunds (Ch. 7), or Should vs. Have to / Must (Ch. 6). However, less advanced learners could benefit from some grammar points, such as Comparative/Superlative (Ch. 3 and 4), or the Vocabulary and Idioms/Expressions sections.

b. The scripts provide real-use examples of the Grammar Focus grammar points, as well as many others that would naturally occur in any English text, such as Regular and Irregular Past Tense Verbs. Students should be encouraged and helped to notice and understand real-use instances of these and other grammar points in the scripts.

APPENDIX 2
-
EXTENSION IDEAS

CHAPTER 1
BELLING THE CAT

 **Writing & Discussion Projects**
1. Retell the story so the mice succeed in putting a bell around the cat's neck

Suggestion 1

The mice could buy a beautiful bell and ribbon online (possibly using a credit card they steal from the house's owner) and have it delivered to the house (perhaps with a note that reads, "For your lovely cat from a secret admirer" or perhaps as a prize for wining a contest). The owner takes the bell and puts it around the cat's neck: "How cute my cat looks with the bell around her neck!" The cat protests but the owner doesn't listen to her. The mice are happy.

Suggestion 2

The mice photoshop a picture of Hello Kitty with a bell around her neck. They print it out (or post it on Instagram). The Cat sees her hero (Hello Kitty) with a bell and wants to have one, too. She persuades her owner to buy her one. The mice are happy.

CHAPTER 2
THE SHEPHERD BOY AND THE WOLF

 **Writing & Discussion Projects**
1. Retell the story so that the boy escapes from the wolf.
2. Write a script about the trial of the boy (who wasn't eaten) for being careless and allowing the wolf to eat the sheep.

Suggestion 1

We can also tell the story so that the wolf eats the sheep but doesn't eat the boy.

Suggestion 2

We can write a script where the story is told at the trial of the boy, who is being tried in court for allowing the sheep to be eaten. The characters could be the Boy, the Judge, the Farmers, and maybe a surviving Sheep as a witness.[28]

---

28 This excellent idea was suggested by my trainees Kim Yujin, Seok Wonkyung, Choi Jeongha, Kim Jingeol, and Kim Jihye

CHAPTER 3
THE NORTH WIND AND THE SUN

 ## Writing & Discussion Projects

2. Is persuasion always better than force? Think of a situation where the wind's way is better. Retell the story so that the Wind wins.

3. Retell the story of the wind and the sun in a school setting who could be the wind and sun? What couldthe contest be about?

Suggestion 2

The story could go as it does in the original story and script, with the sun winning and saying, "Persuasion is better than force." Then the story could continue. The wind expresses regret about losing, the sun boasts about being stronger, when suddenly a large swarm of bees or wasps heads toward the traveler to attack him/her. The traveler could cry for help, or another character (Cloud?) could say, "Help him/her, Sun! You're the strongest!" The sun could shine brightly, with no effect on the bees. Then the wind could say, "Let me try!" The story could end when the wind blows the bees away and everyone realizes that sometimes force is better than persuasion, or that everyone has his/her own strengths.

Suggestion 3

The wind could be a student who tries to be popular by bullying other students.

CHAPTER 4
THE RABBIT AND THE TURTLE

 **Writing & Discussion Projects**
2. Retell the story in a school setting. What could the race or contest be about? Who could be the rabbit? Who could be the turtle?

Suggestion 2

Rather than a race, the contest could be an English Speech Contest. One student ("the Rabbit") has parents that send him/her to a private academy. They also send him/her abroad to Canada every summer for English study. He/She brags about how good his/her English skills are. Another student ("the Turtle") doesn't go to a private academy and has never been abroad. The "Rabbit" student is overconfident and doesn't work hard on the English Speech. The "Turtle" student works hard and wins the contest.

Bibliography

Ahn, Eun-ok (2012). Effects of Creative Thinking Enhancing Activities on Underachievers in Technical High School. Thesis for the Degree of Master, Department of TESOL, The Graduate School, Sookmyung Women's University.

Ausubel, David P. (1967). "Learning Theory and Classroom Practice," Ontario Institute for Studies in Education Bulletin, Vol 1.

Desiatova, Liubov (2009). "Using Different Forms of Drama in the EFL Classroom." Humanizing Language Teaching Magazine 4 (August).

Dörnyei, Zoltán (2010). Motivational Strategies in the Language Classroom. Cambridge University Press.

Goleman, Daniel (2005). Emotional Intelligence, 10th Anniversary Edition. New York, Random House.

Kagan. S. and Kagan. M. (2009). Cooperative Learning. San Clemente, CA : Kagan Publishing.

Kang, Nam Joon (2017). "Use of Personal Analogy for Young Learners' English Language Learning" in The New Studies of English Language and Literature, No. 66, pp.55-77.

Krashen, Steven D. (2004). "Applying the Comprehension Hypothesis: Some Suggestions." Paper presented at the 13th International Symposium and Book Fair on Language Teaching (English Teachers Association of the Republic of China), Taipei, Taiwan, November, 13.

Moore, Kenneth H. and Erik Figueroa (2012). "Reader's Theater in Mixed-Skill Classrooms: Guidelines for Writing Effective Reader's Theater Scripts," KOTESOL International Conference, Seoul, October 21.

Schmidt, Richard W. (1990). "The Role of Consciousness in Second Language Learning." Applied Linguistics, Vol. 11, No. 2, 129-158.

Shepard, Aaron (2004). Readers on Stage: Resources for Reader's Theater. Los Angeles: Shepard Publications.

Sousa, David A. (2006). How the Brain Learns. Thousand Oaks, CA: Corwin Press.

Starko, Alane Jordan (2010). Creativity in the Classroom, 4th Edition.
New York and London: Routledge.

Swain, Merrill (1995). "Three Functions of Output in Foreign Language Learning."
In Guy Cook and Barbara Seidlhofer (Eds.),
Principle and Practice in Applied Linguistics: Studies in Honour of H G.
Widdowson. Oxford University Press.

Zyoud, Munther (2010). "Using Drama Activities and Techniques to Foster

Teaching English as a Foreign Language: a Theoretical Perspective."

**Dr. Moore's
Reading and Writing Series**

New Aesop's
Fable Scripts

초판 1쇄	2018년 4월 25일
지은이	Kenneth H. Moore
펴낸이	홍민기
디자인	REDSEA
펴낸곳	위민북스
	출판등록 제 2018-000030 호
	문의 wemeanbooks@gmail.com
ISBN	979-11-963634-0-6 13740

* 이 도서의 판권은 위민북스와 저자인 Kenneth H. Moore에 있습니다.
  이 도서의 전부 혹은 일부를 재사용하려면 반드시 양측의 서면 동의를 받아야 합니다.

* 이 도서의 국립중앙도서관 출판예정도서목록(CIP)은 서지정보유통지원시스템 홈페이지 (http://seoji.nl.go.kr)와
  국가자료공동목록시스템 (http://www.nl.go.kr/kolisnet)에서 이용하실 수 있습니다. (CIP제어번호 : CIP2018011573)